HOSPITALIT ACCOUNTING

Hospitality Finance and Accounting provides a uniquely concise, accessible and comprehensive introduction to hospitality, finance and accounting from a managerial perspective. By avoiding unnecessary jargon and focusing on the essentials, this book offers a crucial breakdown of an often overly-complex subject area. The concise chapters cover the essential concepts, ideas and formulas to be mastered within the hospitality industry, including income statements, balance sheets, pricing and budgeting.

Each chapter is split into two sections: theory and practice, giving students a practical insight into the everyday realities of the hospitality industry. Emphasis is placed particularly on the practices of operating and capital budget management within the lodging, events, and food and beverage industry.

This new second edition has been updated with:

- A new case study and practice material from Asia.
- New content on event management, cost-volume-profit analysis (break-even), and information asymmetry.
- An updated hotel income statement format to conform to the new 12th edition of the Uniform System of Accounts for the Lodging Industry (USALI).

Rob van Ginneken teaches Finance and Accounting at the Academy of Hotel Management, Breda University of applied sciences in the Netherlands.

Hospitality Essentials Series
Series Editor: Roy C. Wood, School of Tourism, Events and Hospitality Management, Leeds Beckett University, UK

Hotel Accommodation Management
Edited by Roy C. Wood

Strategic Questions in Food and Beverage Management
Roy C. Wood

Improving Sustainability in the Hospitality Industry
Frans Melissen and Lieke Sauer

Managing People in the Hospitality Industry
Michael Riley

Hospitality Finance and Accounting
Rob van Ginneken

Hospitality Finance and Accounting, 2nd Edition
Edited by Rob van Ginneken

For more information about this series, please visit: www.routledge.com/Hospitality-Essentials-Series/book-series/RHE

HOSPITALITY FINANCE AND ACCOUNTING

Second Edition

Edited by Rob van Ginneken

Routledge
Taylor & Francis Group
LONDON AND NEW YORK

Designed cover image: Getty Images

Second edition published 2026
by Routledge
4 Park Square, Milton Park, Abingdon, Oxon OX14 4RN

and by Routledge
605 Third Avenue, New York, NY 10158

Routledge is an imprint of the Taylor & Francis Group, an informa business

First edition published by Routledge 2019

British Library Cataloguing-in-Publication Data
A catalogue record for this book is available from the British Library

ISBN: 9781032900377 (hbk)
ISBN: 9781032900391 (pbk)
ISBN: 9781003545903 (ebk)

DOI: 10.4324/9781003545903

Typeset in Garamond
by Apex CoVantage, LLC

Access the Support Material: www.routledge.com/9781032900391

Contents

List of Figures

List of tables

List of contributors

Michael Dutnall, MCA is the Executive Chef of White's, the oldest gentlemen's club in London, UK. Starting his career as an apprentice in five-star hotel The Connaught, he later worked in equally prestigious restaurants, hotels and, prior to joining White's, the Royal Airforce Club, all in London. In 2009, he achieved one of the greatest accolades in the culinary world, the Master of Culinary Arts.

Agatha Engel is a Certified Public Accountant and has been teaching Accounting to students in the United States and in Europe for more than 15 years. Currently she is an internal auditor using her accounting enthusiasm in-company.

Rob van Ginneken teaches Finance and Accounting in the Hotel Management program at Breda University of Applied Sciences, The Netherlands. His special interest is ownership, operating and branding models in the international hotel industry. Rob also holds the Wine & Spirit Education Trust Diploma in Wine and Spirits, and is a Certified Educator for WSET certifications level 1, 2 and 3.

Jur van de Graaf is a Management Team member and lecturer Accounting & Operations Management at the Academy for Leisure & Events, Breda University of applied sciences, The Netherlands. His main interest is automating (financial) management information and creating management reports.

James W. Hesford, PhD, now retired, spent twenty-six years as an accounting professor in business and hospitality schools in the United States, Switzerland and Canada. His main interests are in managerial accounting, specifically cost management and management control in the hospitality industry.

John Mackillop is currently retired from his position as a Lecturer in Economics and Managerial Accounting at Breda University of Applied Sciences, The Netherlands. He also taught in the MBA in Global Hospitality Management at Les Roches, Switzerland, and in management schools in Scotland, Canada and Switzerland.

Craig M. Milner, MBA, is Senior Lecturer in Management and Organizational Studies at the Dhillon School of Business, University of Lethbridge in Calgary, Canada. Prior to the Dhillon School, he accumulated more than 20 years of management experience at General Motors, Procter and Gamble, and Frito-Lay. Craig also owned and operated a restaurant where he honed his interest and passion for organizational performance and high-performance teams.

Michael J. Turner, PhD, is a Senior Lecturer in Accounting at the UQ Business School, The University of Queensland in Brisbane, Australia, where he currently serves as the Program Convenor for the Bachelor of Advanced Business with Honours. His research and teaching specialization is in hospitality managerial accounting focusing on capital expenditure decision-making, competition, strategy, and the strategic partnerships between hotel owners, management companies and general managers, and the ensuing performance implications.

Han Yu, PhD, is a Lecturer-Researcher in the College of Finance and Economics at Sichuan International Studies University, Chongqing, China. Specializing in green finance, she researches how ESG performance affects corporate financing and overall organizational performance.

Preface

Wowing guests by exceeding their expectations (yes, this is how people in the industry talk) is generally only worth doing if it can be done *profitably*. With this book, we aim to support you in whatever may be your career objectives, by helping you develop into financially competent hospitality professionals. Fear not: "financially competent" does not mean this book will teach you how to do bookkeeping. If you go on to study other accounting texts after this one, you will notice that all of the authors make more or less this same claim. Most of them then go on to prove themselves wrong, introducing and discussing in detail many accounting principles, complicated methods for allocating overhead, a myriad of ways to depreciate assets, exceptions to the rules, and so on, and so forth. But becoming financially competent does not require you to know all of the above. It is much more important to develop a sound grasp of *the essentials*. The aim of this book is to deliver a truly "Essentials Only" work to serve as the starting point for the Accounting curriculum, and something faculty and students can further build on.

A word of comfort for those who feel uneasy about their numerical skills. Finance and Accounting are really more of a language than about numbers. It is in fact the language in which knowledgeable people discuss the well-being of an organization. "Yes, but only from a financial point of view", we hear you say. But can you imagine saying anything about an organization that can *not* be put in financial terms? You might ask the maître d' of a hotel restaurant how well it is doing. He may answer that it's doing fine as it is almost always fully booked. But is it also making money? Is he aware of the huge costs for personnel? Is he selling the right meals and wines (the ones which contribute not only to the gastronomic guest experience, but also to profit)? Is the restaurant open for lunch and if so, is that cost effective? The Marketing and Sales executive, being asked the same question, will inform you of the latest full colour brochure she has developed, and the growing number of foreign guests staying in the hotel. But can she also vouch for the fact that the rooms are sold at a reasonable average rate – and what that rate would be? And if so, how about the revenue per available room?

This is the language my fellow contributors and I would like to teach you. Speaking it competently means you can take the right *decisions*. Take investment decisions, for example. Is it wise to expand the hotel's banqueting capacity? Someone would need to make assumptions about increasing revenues and weigh these against the costs associated with the expansion. Just as in a language, where you have to stick to certain grammar rules in order to make sense, Finance and Accounting offer you the right structure to correctly answer investment questions.

One last remark: many textbooks make quite a fuss about what is actually "Finance", what "Financial Accounting", and what constitutes "Managerial Accounting". The gist of it seems to be that Finance relates specifically to how a business is financed; Financial Accounting is concerned with producing external reports to for example shareholders or the tax authorities, and Managerial Accounting aims to provide management with tools to help them take decisions that make business sense. In this book, we will use the terms much more liberally, and use "Finance and Accounting" as a more generic expression for all financial concepts managers need to understand. And as these concepts are often closely linked, a study tip would be to go back and forth between chapters, and benefit from the different ways in which the authors approach the subjects.

We hope you have fun learning this new language!

Notes on the second edition

In this second edition, the overall structure of the book has remained intact. Errors have been corrected and where necessary, the text has been updated. Following a recommendation from the reviewers we included a discussion of financial management in the context of Events Management – the new Practice section of Chapter 3. Michael Dutnall wrote an epilogue to his "Diary of an executive chef" – the Practice section of Chapter 4 in this and in the first edition – to share how his job has changed now that the world looks so different, in many ways, from that of 2018.

Acknowledgements

I would like to thank a number of people who have been instrumental in getting this second edition to press. First of all Emma Travis, Commissioning Editor, for encouraging me to produce a second edition, and second, the anonymous reviewers of the first edition, who suggested valuable changes. Emma's colleague Sarah Lewis has been a great help in sorting out operational and admin tasks.

I believe it takes an expert to explain the essentials of something, so I am extremely glad my contributors agreed to write or edit their parts of the book. Welcome and thanks to new contributors Jur de Graaf, for writing the Practice section on Event Management, and to Han Yu for "adopting" and updating John Mackillop's Pricing chapter after his retirement.

The practice section of the first chapter has been anonymized; that of the last chapter is fictive, but heavily based on a number of real-life investment cases. I can't name and thank the managers involved in helping me write these sections here, but you know who you are, and rest assured: I am very grateful for your cooperation.

Rob van Ginneken
Tilburg, May 2025

CHAPTER

1 Measuring performance

Learning outcomes

At the end of this chapter, readers should:

- appreciate the importance of measuring financial performance, for any business but especially for the hospitality industry;
- understand essential accounting principles and the general structure of an income statement to correctly interpret this report;
- be familiar with the most important sources of revenue and expenses in a hospitality business;
- understand how hospitality managers monitor actual versus past performance and versus the operating budget, using simple techniques such as vertical and horizontal analysis.

THEORY

Rob van Ginneken

Introduction: Two financial perspectives

Basically, there are two ways to look at any business from a financial perspective. One way, which we will explore in more detail in Chapter 2, focuses on what a business *owns* and *owes* at a certain moment in time. Think of the amount of cash in the organization: the petty cash in the secretaries' office, in cash registers in departments where money is received from customers, or the money in bank accounts. Or imagine the value of the buildings, furniture, operating supplies and inventories. Or, in terms of what the business owes: money it may have borrowed and needs to pay back over time. You can hopefully imagine businesses would want to keep track of all of these. It's a bit like taking a photograph of the organization; that is also a reflection of the way things are *at a moment in time*. The photograph in question is actually the financial statement known as the *balance sheet*, or *the statement of financial position*.

DOI: 10.4324/9781003545903-1

The other way of looking at a business from a financial point of view is arguably much more interesting for those interested in a career in hospitality management. This perspective is more like filming to track the *activities* and *results* (financial performance) of a business over time. In financial terms, you look at how operations lead to the organization becoming either richer or poorer: the business provides guests with a meal and receives payment for that; pays its employees salaries in return for their labour; and experiences a decreasing value, over time, of equipment, to name but a few factors. Hospitality firms typically do this on a daily basis: restaurant owners, hotel management teams, club managers, they all like to track the performance of their business day in, day out.

There are different names for the financial report that measures financial performance. If the report is about performance in a *past* period (yesterday, last month, last quarter etc.) it is often called the (daily, monthly, etc.) *income statement*, or *profit and loss account*. If the report is about the expected or desired results in a *future* period, it is often called the operating budget. A budget is a financial plan. You can learn more about operating budgets, and how management monitors real performance versus the budgeted one, in the practice part of this chapter. Chapter 4 discusses the *cash* budget, a related but different kind of budget. After studying the next section of the current chapter, you may already appreciate the difference between the two.

It may help to compare the two financial perspectives to the movie "Super Size Me". The movie is about the protagonist eating three daily meals at McDonald's for an entire month. Apparently, Mr. Spurlock had a fat percentage of 11% at the start of the 30-day period, and of 18% at the end. These fat percentages could be seen as balance sheet data: the 11 and 18 convey information about his situation (how much fat he has) at a certain moment in time. The movie itself, spanning the 30 days of his experiment, would be the income statement: we would see how much weight he gained (by eating burgers and fries, and drinking sodas) and how much he lost (by walking from his car to the restaurant, for example). Obviously, there is a link between these two perspectives: the excessive eating and drinking, and lack of any serious physical exercise probably *caused* the increase in fat percentage. In financial terms: if a business performs well in a period (i.e. the income statement will look great), that will also show on the next balance sheet. We will discuss how this works in the next chapter.

The Income Statement and two "accounting principles"

Revenues and expenses are what's on an income statement. Roughly speaking, revenue is the value of what you have sold in a given period, and expenses are the costs incurred in doing business in that period. Not only of the costs of the materials involved, but also the costs of labour (people you had to pay to make the product or provide the service or do the administration or supervise other people), of rent you had to pay for the premises, interest you had to pay on a loan etc., etc. – unfortunately for business owners, the list is long! If you put revenues and expenses (we'll go into more detail about those two shortly) in one statement, and subtract expenses from revenue, you have what's called profit.

The more successful a business is in a) selling its products and services and b) running a tight ship (in other words, in keeping expenses in line with revenue), the more profitable it will be. In accounting terms: the more revenue (the "top line" on an income statement) will end up being profit (which is "the bottom line"). In hospitality businesses, this is often referred to as the "flow-through"; in the practice part of this chapter you will see an example of how a hotel management team discusses this. Of course, it is also possible – but clearly not desirable! – that expenses exceed revenue in a certain period. The business is then said to have a loss for that period.

At this point, it is important to make sure you understand revenue for a period is not necessarily the exact amount of money received in that period from clients. Nor do total expenses always equal all payments made. Revenues and expenses are on an income statement, and they reflect the business successes of a firm, in terms of value gained or lost. Cash receipts and cash disbursements (a posh way of saying "payments") may be the result of revenues and expenses but express something different. A few examples to illustrate this point.

Let's say a restaurant hosts a wedding party on 15 June. The party over, the restaurant has provided the newly-weds with a service and goods (food and beverages); as a result, the guests now owe the restaurant money. The owner includes this as revenue in her income statement for June, even if the couple would not be expected to pay until July or even August. This is referred to as the *recognition* principle. In other words, the cash will be received later, but the business can "recognize" and report it delivered a service, and thus record this as revenue in June. The same is true for expenses versus payments. Let's say the crew of a cruise ship put in a lot of overtime in a certain month in high season. Even if the overtime may only be paid out next month, this is an expense which will be put in the month the hours were worked. This second important accounting principle is known as the *matching* principle. The idea is that to correctly assess performance in a given period, you subtract from revenue in that period all expenses which should be matched, are linked to that revenue, regardless of when they were paid for.

If all of this may sound overly complicated, just as often as not revenues and receipts *do* go hand in hand, as do expenses and payments – many customers pay straight away, employers pay regular July salaries in July, etc. There are, however, a few other situations in which expenses and cash disbursements do not go hand in hand. Let's say a hotel buys a laptop to be used by the Banqueting Department. Is this an expense for the current accounting period? An expense, as we have seen earlier, is a loss of value needed to generate revenue. But can we really speak of a loss of value? The answer is "no", as in effect we have traded one possession (an "asset") for another – cash for a laptop. So we have not lost any value. That is to say, not at the time of the purchase. The matching principle applies here in the sense that we *spread out* the total cost of the laptop over the period in which it is of use to us. This expense is called depreciation (colloquially, this is often referred to as "writing off" the laptop), and, following the matching principle, will impact the income statement.

One more example: a business has borrowed money (for example to buy the laptop mentioned above) and now makes a loan payment to the bank. Is this an expense for the current accounting period? No. What is the business losing in value from paying *back* part of a loan? Exactly nothing! They are simply giving back something they just had the temporary use of. Let's take this example one step further and now take into consideration the bank is also a business, and is not content simply lending money and getting it back over time. Somehow, they will expect to get back more than they lent, and the "more" is called interest. To the borrowing company, this interest would be the expense associated with the loan.

At this point, you may ask yourself *how* businesses write off assets, or how much interest they owe the bank in a certain accounting period. It is outside the scope of this "Essentials" text to discuss this in-depth but to give you a first idea, the end of this chapter has a short introductory section on the topic.

Other types of expenses and structure of the income statement

We already discussed some expense types in the rather theoretical section above. Let's have a more practical look at the different kinds of expenses hospitality businesses incur.

By and large, most of the income statements that companies draw up follow a similar "path" going from revenue to profit. The first group of expenses subtracted from revenue is comprised of those expenses most closely linked to actual business operations. How much is the business paying for the products, or the parts thereof, they are selling? How much to pay production personnel?

A second category of expenses would be a bit further removed from actual operations, but still considered "operating expenses" in accounting speak: how about costs of Marketing and Sales, like a social media campaign, how about the expenses of the HR and ICT Department? And how about utilities expenses (the bills received from gas, water and electricity companies)?

The last type of expenses would include, for example, property taxes, rent payable to the company's landlord, or the depreciation and interest expenses discussed briefly earlier. This last group are called non-operating expenses – if you take a close look at them, you'll notice these expenses are more the result of certain choices made by the owner than they are related to how much business the company happens to be doing in a certain accounting period. Did the owners choose to rent a modern, luxurious office building or opt for cheaper yet fully functional premises? Did they have the company borrow as much as possible – causing it to incur a high interest expense – rather than putting a bit more of their own money in the firm?

Your lecturer may talk to you about abbreviations such as EBIT and EBITDA. These relate to different profit levels where certain expenses *have*, and others *have not yet* been subtracted from revenue (e.g. EBITDA stands for Earnings (another word for profit) Before Interest, Taxes, Depreciation and Amortization, whereas EBIT is (you guessed it) Earnings Before Interest and Taxes – a profit level a bit further down the income statement, after the depreciation and amortization expenses have also been subtracted). The last step on the path from revenue to profit is corporate income taxes. Just like personal income (from salaries, or from other sources) is taxed, so are the profits of a business. And so finally we arrive at the bottom line of the income statement: net income or net profit, after taxes.

In the next section, we will introduce the income statement format used by most hotels around the globe – the so-called Uniform System of Accounts for the Lodging Industry (USALI for short). Figure 1.1 shows it closely follows the general set-up of income statements just discussed. Other hospitality operations, such as restaurants or clubs, may use different lay-outs, but once you understand the structure of the USALI format, you will also be able to understand these.

USALI presents us with a three-part income statement.[1] The first (top) part shows all departmental revenues, that is revenues from selling 1) rooms, 2) food and beverage, 3) revenue from other operated departments (think: spa, golf course) and 4) something called "miscellaneous income" – e.g. extra cleaning fees charged for smoking in a non-smoking room. For each of the four departments we then subtract departmental revenues, to arrive at the department's profit or loss – more about that in the next section.

The second and third parts only have expenses. The second part has all the undistributed operating expenses – quite a mouthful for all expenses of what are called by some "service centres", or by others "overhead departments". Whatever the name, the idea is to express that no revenue is generated in and by these departments, but they are essential to the success of the business. The five are: Administrative and General, Information and Telecommunication Systems, Sales and Marketing, Property Operation and Maintenance, and Energy, Water and Waste. The resulting profit after subtracting from revenue all expenses in these two parts is called GOP, or Gross Operating Profit – a very important term in the industry as you will see in a minute!

	Revenue	(Cost of Sales)	(Labor Costs and Related Expenses)	(Other Expenses)	Income (Loss)
Operated departments					
Rooms					
Food and Beverage					
Other Operated Departments	Section 1: Revenue and Expenses of Operating Departments				
Miscellaneous income					
TOTAL Operating revenue					
Undistributed Operating Expenses					
Administrative and General					
Information and Telecommunications Systems	Section 2: Expenses of Service Departments				
Sales and Marketing					
Property Operation and Maintenance					
Energy, Water and Waste					
TOTAL Undistributed Expenses					
Gross Operating Profit					
Management Fees					
Income Before Non-Operating Income and Expenses					
Non-Operating Income and Expenses					
(Non-Operating) Income					
Rent					
Property and Other Taxes					
Insurance					
Other	Section 3: Management fees, Non-Operating Income and Other Expenses				
Earnings Before Interest, Taxes, Depreciation and Amortization					
Interest					
Depreciation					
Amortization					
Income Before Income Taxes					
Income Taxes					
Net Income					

Figure 1.1 USALI 12th Revised Edition overview

The third and last part of our overview shows management fees (payable by the hotel to a management company if the owners have hired a brand or independent management company to run the hotel on their behalf); and non-operating income and expenses. Subtracting all of these expenses and income tax from GOP gives us a hotel's net income.

Let's zoom in on the departmental revenues and expenses part first. The revenue of each department is simply the product of the number of products or services sold to guests, and the selling price of these, excluding any city tax and value-added tax. A hotel with 100 rooms, an occupancy rate of 75% in the month of January, and an average rate of $135 excluding taxes, would have a rooms revenue of 100 × 31 × 0.75 × $135, or $313,875 that month. Moving on to department expenses, the summary statement will show only the totals for this for each department. For each of them, USALI provides hotels with a supporting schedule where department expenses are reported in much more detail. Important types of direct departmental expenses include Cost of Sales (if the department has any), Labour Costs and Related Expenses (all salaries and associated expenses for staff working in that department) and Other Expenses.

For a factory producing bicycles, this Cost of Sales would be the cost for the tires, frame, brakes etc. In hospitality, one or more tangible products are often part of the service, such as in food and beverage operations. In other chapters this expense type will be dealt with in more managerial depth. The rooms department does not have a cost of sales – we are not actually selling the physical room, are we?

The hospitality industry being a very labour-intensive one, labour costs and related expenses are probably the number one expense for many employers. The expense is the salary (or wages) paid, plus any add-on costs such as social security premiums, employee taxes, benefits such as holiday pay, the use of a company car or health insurance, to name a few. The size of these depends, amongst other things, on the industry and the type of collective labour agreement (if any) that applies, the country and the type of position (think management bonus plans). Other departmental expenses vary by department and can be monitored by analysing the support schedules. To give you an idea, "Other Expenses" for the Rooms Department include costs of cleaning supplies, guest room decorations and guest transportation.

In the undistributed operating expenses part of the Income Statement, Administrative and General includes general management related expenses, and expenses of the HR department, but also credit card commissions and charitable or other donations – and many more. Please check the detailed schedules in USALI for more information. The next two, Information and Telecommunication Systems, and Sales and Marketing, sort of speak for themselves. Property Operations and Maintenance includes e.g. engineering supplies and grounds maintenance and landscaping expenses. Energy, Water and Waste, as mentioned before, refers to cost of electricity, gas, sewer and waste services.

The non-operating part of the income statement typically contains some large numbers. Most hospitality businesses operate from some kind of real estate, i.e. a building. Even if they don't (think food trucks, for example) these businesses will use assets (in this case, the truck) which will cost them money in some way, shape or form: the depreciation discussed earlier, if they own the asset; rent, if they lease it; interest on a loan taken out to purchase the asset. In this section of the statement are also taxes. Owning as well as using real estate is taxed in most countries. Hospitality business may also need to get certain permits and licenses from the authorities, for example to serve liquor – taxes in disguise. A small aside: please note that not *all* taxes are in the income statement. Hospitality businesses are also expected to pay tourist tax and sales or value-added tax (VAT) but these are amounts you add to the guest bill, it is *them* paying the tax. Suppose a spa treatment is charged to the guest's bill for $115 including 6% VAT. How much revenue does this mean for the business? Indeed: $115 / 1.06 = $108.49.

All in all, this third and last part of the statement can make for a large difference between GOP and net income. That said, management of a hotel is often not too concerned with this part. Non-operating expenses are mostly a function of investment and financing decisions taken by the developers and owners of a hotel, and as such are largely outside the control of day-to-day management. The latter tend to, and arguably should focus on the things that *are* within their control, which is generating healthy levels of revenue and controlling operating expenses.

Numbers, numbers . . . how to make sense of them?

All in all, a lot of numbers are featured on an income statement. The important question is: how to make sense of them? How to assess whether, in a given accounting period, the business has achieved an acceptable result? And what kind of result should we consider? Not only revenue, so much should be clear by now. Focussing on the bottom line, so on net income, may make sense, as that is indeed the value created by the business for the owner(s). However, each of the lines between revenue and profit may be relevant and interesting. It depends on who you are and what you want to know. In the practice part of this chapter a hotel management team study a monthly income statement in detail. For now, a few comments on what hospitality managers are normally concerned with.

Operated departments: Sales mix and profitability

The term sales mix is used in hospitality and other businesses to break down total revenue into (in this case) the extent to which each of the departments brings in revenue. The sales mix could be represented in a pie chart form – each department would generate a slice of the pie. In a hotel, expect the Rooms Department to generate most revenue; in a cinema, it's probably ticket sales. What both examples have in common, is that the marginal cost of an extra guest or visitor is low – the costs of running a hotel, or showing a movie, hardly increase with the number of guests/visitors. On the other hand, an empty guest or banqueting room, or an empty cinema seat, is a revenue opportunity not realised. The managerial lesson: as long as you can charge a reasonable room rate/ticket price, make sure the guest rooms and theatre are full, each day, every day.

In both examples, other operated departments, such as Food and Beverage, may generate a healthy additional revenue stream. An important analysis could be whether this also contributes to overall *profit*. The author is no cinema expert, but he could well imagine how movie-goers buying expensive popcorn and soft drinks, to enjoy during the movie and sold to them in a simple and well-organised "over the counter" way, would have a much larger flow-through than the complex F&B operations in a hotel. In the latter, guests may decide to skip (and not pay for) breakfast, or not have it in the hotel; lunch-time may well see a near-empty restaurant – and bored-to-death waiters and chefs who still expect to receive full pay at the end of the month. Check out the "Finance and Accounting in F&B" chapter, Chapter 4, and especially the practice part "Diary of an Executive Chef" for a better idea of how challenging it is to make money in F&B.

In practice, management will have established targets for revenue and expenses. This brings us to the following point.

Percentages

Especially internally used income statements will express many of the figures on it as percentages, too, which can really help management make sense of the absolute amounts. The sales mix we just discussed is a first example: a hotel management team may monitor what percentage of total revenue comes from rooms, how much from F&B, and so on. If rooms revenue is generally between 70 and 75% and drops to 68% in a given month, that may be a reason to investigate further. Obviously, in this case there may not be a reason for concern – it may well mean the other departments had an exceptionally good month!

Using percentages is also helpful for monitoring expense levels. Just looking at the absolute expense amounts can easily lead to the wrong conclusions. As you can probably appreciate, if revenues increase, total expenses typically also increase. More diners in your restaurant also mean a higher food cost. More "heads in beds" means a higher housekeeping expense. In absolute terms, that is. That's why expense *percentages* are often used in analysing financial performance. Each expense line item is expressed as a percentage of either total, or a specific department's revenue. The food cost percentage would be the food cost of sales, expressed as a percentage of total food revenue. The labour expense percentage: total (or a specific operated department's) labour and related expenses expressed as a percentage of total (or the department's) revenue. To interpret the percentages, management compares the percentages to the desired, or target percentage. An important part of becoming financially literate, is knowing what kind of targets are realistic for a specific hospitality operation. A family restaurant will generate different food and beverage cost percentages than a three Michelin star restaurant. The labour expense percentage of a limited service budget hotel can't be compared to that of a full-service upscale property. More about expense ratios in the "Pricing" and "Finance and Accounting in F&B" chapters.

What can be said about expenses is also true for profit levels. For example: managers and owners will track not only absolute levels of GOP, but also expect this to be at least a certain percentage of revenue. The word used for this kind of percentage is "margin". Let's say the GOP margin target for a property is 30%, this means at least 30 cents of every dollar of revenue is supposed to become gross operating profit. Net profit margin is the term used for net income as a percentage of revenue. Are you wondering how much bottom line profit a hotel owner can expect? Of course, this is heavily dependent on, for example, the general state of the economy and corporate tax rates, but as an indication one of the largest hotel owners in the world, HOST Hotels & Resorts (2024, 2021), reported a net income of $752 million in 2023, and revenue of $5,311 million, meaning a net profit margin of 14.2%. Please mind that three years earlier, in Covid19-stricken 2020, these numbers were –$741 and $1,620 respectively, in other words a net profit margin of *minus* 45.7%!

The above use of percentages is often referred to as common-size, or vertical analysis – expressing a figure (in this case an income statement line item) as a percentage of the bigger whole, of something further up the financial statement (revenue). The name suggests there may also be something like *horizontal* analysis, and there is. Horizontal refers to comparing financial data *in time*. If last year's labour expense was $7,750,002 and this year's $8,119,988, that corresponds to an increase of 4.8%. Is this in fact a negative development that should have management worried? Well, perhaps not. What if revenue increased from $19,620,253 last year to $21,368,421 this year? That would actually constitute an *improvement* in the labour expense percentage from 39.5% (7,750,002 / 19,620,253 × 100%) to 38% (8,119,988 / 21,368,421 × 100%). Combining vertical and horizontal analysis, we could say the labour expense percentage improved by 3.8% this year ((39.5–38) / 39.5 × 100%). Savvy?

Table 1.1 Horizontal and vertical analysis

	This year	*Last year*	*Percentage change*
Revenue	21,368,421	19,620,253	8.9%
Payroll expense	8,119,988	7,750,002	4.8%
	38%	39.5%	

Loan amortization and Depreciation 101

As promised, this chapter ends with a short introduction to the workings of two concepts discussed earlier: how do businesses deal with debt (loans) and how do they depreciate assets?

Loan amortization and interest

Interest is the price paid (or received) for borrowing (or from lending) money. How do borrowers pay lenders back, and how is interest calculated? There are many different ways, and, basically, it's up to whatever the two parties agree to. In this primer, let's look at what is called straight-line amortization. Amortization refers to the paying back of a loan over time, and straight-line means that the amount of debt outstanding decreases at a constant pace over time. That is, the borrower pays back the money in equal instalments over time.

So, how to calculate these instalment and interest payments, then? Instalment is easy: just divide the total loan to be repaid by the number of payments. $100,000 to be repaid over 20 years, at the end of each year? The instalment is $5,000 per year. Calculating interest in a straight-line amortization case is not rocket science either. You only need to consider that the interest rate is based on borrowing a certain amount for a period of one year, and expresses the percentage of the amount borrowed that you need to pay.

An illustration:

> A business borrows $100,000 for one year, to be amortized straight-line in 12 monthly payments, with a 6% annual interest rate. Instalment each month: $100,000 / 12 = $8,333. The interest payable at the end of the first month will be $100,000 × 0.06 × 1 / 12 = $500.
>
> How much interest will be payable at the end of the second month? During that second month, the balance of the loan is $100,000 *less* the first instalment of $8,333 = $91,667. This means the interest due at, and for this second month, is $91,667 × 0.06 / 12 = $458.

So far for "loan amortization 101".

Let's move on to depreciation.

Depreciation

Depreciation is arguably one of the most abstract and difficult to understand concepts in Accounting. Some instructors explain it using the "savings" approach: the company sets aside money for the eventual replacement of a fixed asset (one the business will be using for more than one year) after it has become economically obsolete. This is rather confusing: the company might not actually save for the replacement, as it may very well be possible to pay for the new fixed asset from the regular operating cash flow. Or it may borrow money in order to do so.

The only proper way to explain what depreciation is, is through the matching principle discussed earlier. It states that you should match the costs of an asset with the revenues being generated by it. This means that if an airline intends to fly their newly-acquired airplane for 30 years, it will spread out the purchase price it paid over that period. This makes sense, as you could say that by buying the plane, they actually bought a certain "flying capacity", a capacity you could measure in flying hours – let's say 30 years at 11.5 months a year at 80% "air time" equals more or less 200,000 hours. And doesn't it make sense to acknowledge those costs as they are made, that is, as those 200,000 hours are *used up*? In other words, you match the flying hours with the associated flights that create the revenue.

Let's move on to the practical side of depreciation: how do you decide how much to write off each period? Just as with the amortization of loans as just discussed, the simplest method is straight-line depreciation: each accounting period the business writes off the same amount. How much exactly, depends on the *useful life* of the fixed asset, and on the residual value it is expected to have at the end of its useful life. The useful life is simply how long the business expects to use the asset before replacing it by a new one. The annual depreciation is then the difference between the purchase price and the residual value, divided by the number of years in the useful life.

An illustration:

> A laptop, bought for $800, has a useful life of 4 years and is expected to have a residual value of $50. The business would then report a depreciation expense of ($800 – $50) / 4 = $750 / 4 = $187.50 per year.

Just as with loan amortization, "straight-line" is only the simplest, most basic method; many others exist in real life, with intriguing names like "sum of the years' digits" and "declining balance". Most regular accounting texts will discuss at least one of them.

Conclusion

Hospitality businesses, perhaps more so than other types of companies, put a very heavy managerial focus on monitoring operating performance. Certain characteristics, such as the labour and capital intense nature of the industry, make that "bottom-line" profit is by no means guaranteed. This chapter has shed some light on a few fundamental concepts you need to be familiar with. The practice part will provide you with a sneak peek behind the scenes of an internationally branded hotel. More specifically, it essentially consists of the minutes of the monthly P&L (income statement) meeting, in which management discuss performance last month, year-to-date, and look ahead to the next few months.

Bibliography

Ginneken, Rob van (2013). Income Statements in Hospitality Finance. In Roy C. Wood, *Hospitality Finance, Key Concepts in Hospitality Management*. London: Sage.

Host Hotels & Resorts (2024). *Host Hotels & Resorts, Inc. Reports Results for 2023*. Available online at https://ir.hosthotels.com/news-releases/news-release-details/host-hotels-resorts-inc-reports-results-2023 (accessed 10 January, 2025).

Host Hotels & Resorts (2021). *Host Hotels & Resorts, Inc. Reports Results for 2020*. Available online at https://ir.hosthotels.com/news-releases/news-release-details/host-hotels-resorts-inc-reports-results-2020 (accessed 10 January, 2025).

HFTP (2024). *Uniform System of Accounts for the Lodging Industry*, 12th Revised Edition. Austin: Hospitality Financial and Technology Professionals.

Schmidgall, Raymond S. (2017). *Hospitality Industry Managerial Accounting*. Lansing: American Hotel & Lodging Educational Institute.

PRACTICE: THE FEBRUARY MONTHLY

Rob van Ginneken

Introduction

This chapter consists of the minutes of a so-called "monthly" meeting. Hotels the world over hold such meetings, in which management discusses the results of the month before. Usually, they also look ahead to the next (few) month(s). The minutes have been shortened and small, mostly name changes have been made to anonymize the text, but otherwise all of it is real. The property in question is a full-service, owner-operated hotel, affiliated through a franchise agreement with one of the large international brands. It is situated in the centre of a large city somewhere in continental Europe.

We hope this kind of "sneak peek behind the scenes" will help you better understand some of the basics of this first chapter. Just reading the text (intently) will tell you a lot about the kinds of things that require hospitality managers' attention. But if you really want to understand the structure and meaning of an income statement, may we suggest as a learning approach that you try to *re-assemble* in USALI format the (main parts of) monthly from these minutes?

The minutes

Financial Controller (FC): OK, the results for February. For the first time in 14 months we did not make budget. That said, total revenue is very good at €876,000, 11% more than last year. A very nice increase, even if under budget. So, I see it as an indication our budget is just ambitious, and perhaps we can't expect to make it each and every month. Year-to-Date (YTD) we are still over budget, so January included we are 1% over.

A quick look down the P&L, at GOP; because what we have been very successful at this month is to keep expenses under control. A few expenses were lower than expected. Of course, it's always a special month, February, what with all the conferences in town and the International Athletic Event (IAE). The associated one-off expenses have of course been budgeted, so the moment they turn out to be less than expected, we keep GOP under control. And we did, the bottom line is that while being €22,000 under our revenue budget, we are just €3,000 under in terms of GOP. So, in January we were nicely *over* budget, GOP-wise, and unfortunately February erased a bit from that. So that's a quick impression of the final result of February.

Revenue Manager (RevMan): In Rooms we did not make the budgeted revenue. Keep in mind February was the month with the largest budgeted increase versus last year. We did manage to get 105K more than last year, so not quite budget but still an OK increase. The main reason for not making budget is the lower-than-expected pick-up of the Large Medical Conference (LMC) group; we expected more from that. We received many high room rate cancellations. If you look at our segmentation, you see quite a few room nights less than budget, 325, and also 250 less than last year. Overall in Transient – individual business – we are 8K over budget; most of this is from [the average daily] rate (ADR), €14 over budget. Good segments were "Corporate", an increase here of €3, and "Other Discount", which includes our long stays, so our guests who stay more than five nights. Here we were €50 over budget, ADR-wise, so that's positive and €62 more than last year, with an extra 100 nights. In Group Corporate we were on budget in terms of nights, but €22 over our ADR budget. In Group Leisure we were 141 nights under budget, mostly because the tour business did not deliver in February. We are also €8 under our ADR budget there. Overall, we are 40 nights short of budget in Groups, but €2 over budget in rate. A bit surprising is that we are growing in occupancy but not in guest numbers, compared to last year. We did an analysis of the IAE and we sold more doubles then. So, all other weeks and periods we received fewer guests per room.

FC: I noticed an average number of guests per room of 1.25 and I seem to remember it was 1.37 last year, indeed the average for the full year being 1.37, so yes, that's lower.

REVMAN: During the IAE it was much higher, we had a lot of double occupancy, and 100 guests more.

FC: And how many nights, compared to last year?

REVMAN: 35 nights more.

FC: And the totals for the LMC, how does that stack up to last year?

REVMAN: I still have to prepare that overview. In the end, the organization block remained flat, it's just that we didn't get as many participants in. In the last two weeks before the conference, the other hotels in town didn't keep their rates high, so as I just mentioned, we got a lot of cancellations of people who went to other hotels.

FC: OK. Let's go to Payroll in Rooms.

ROOMS DIVISION MANAGER (RDM): I have lower expenses in salaried payroll, but we had to employ more hourly workers because of sick leave and team members taking time off in February. That accounts for the budget variance, as we had to schedule people differently. In the Executive Lounge, Etienne, I don't know if you would like to add anything but I'd say we are quite on budget there.. . . Anything worth mentioning?

FOOD AND BEVERAGE MANAGER (FBM): I actually don't get these numbers, but as far as I know results should be exactly on budget.

RDM: They are. But good to know you don't get these figures. Perhaps the results of the [just-opened] Executive Lounge can also be shared with Etienne as he manages these hours even though they sit within my [Rooms Division] concept?

FC: Payroll Housekeeping, Elisabetta, would you like to comment?

HOUSEKEEPING MANAGER (HKM): Yes, we saved €1,000 overall; we had some associates on sick leave but that was more than balanced out by more salaried people taking time off than budgeted; plus I think we scheduled really well.

FC: And, of course, occupancy was a bit lower.

RDM: And a nice average time per room.

HKM: Yes, below the budgeted number of minutes per room.

RDM: The hours for extra security during the IAE, are they also included?

ASSISTANT FINANCIAL CONTROLLER (AFC): Partly. The hours Danny worked in the last week, yes, they are in. The hours during the IAE? No, those are in Administrative and General.

RDM: Good, so total Payroll Rooms in line with budget even though we had lower occupancy. In the controllables, we see a higher laundry expense which is the result of our linen replacement in February. We also expect a credit invoice related to this which will make us on budget again, Year-to-Date. Printing and stationary we ordered in February for our new Executive Lounge. Guest Amenities is under budget because we already took an accrual in February of €2,000. Travel agents commission is lower, which is interesting as this usually only seems to go up . . . also, uniforms this month, we took an accrual in January so no expenses in February. The Executive Lounge gives me the feeling we are "in control" expense wise, looking at the budget. Do you share that feeling?

EXECUTIVE CHEF (EC): Yes, food-wise no excessive expenses for the Lounge and operations appear to go smoothly. We are going to run some numbers on how much we are spending per guest so we can fine-tune our ordering if we have the forecast.

GENERAL MANAGER (GM): I think we have to take into consideration that the IAE week was something special; and with the LMC you'd say usage of the Executive Lounge was very high. Perhaps the two cancel out?

AFC: No, it doesn't. But if we take February and March, next month we'll have two comparisons and will be better able to analyse expense per guest.

FC: By the way, I sent all of you that email this morning to make sure all breakfast cost of sales will be booked in the kitchen cost.

EC: That is the case, and I get the breakfast revenue through the rate code.

GM: Back to the analysis: hotel occupancy is obviously not so important for the forecast; it's about the occupancy of the rooms that have access to the Executive Lounge; so, an overall occupancy of 80% could mean we could close part of the Lounge if there are no high-tier Loyalty Program member guests. Does everyone have that kind of occupancy info?

FC: I feel that the next few months, at the end of March perhaps, we'd have to see which ratios we can use and track each month, to optimize purchasing, for how much goes into it.

RDM: OK, so controllable expenses Rooms is within budget, even a bit under, €18,000 euro, making for a bottom-line Rooms department profit of 66, almost 67 percent.

GM: Which is a great result.

FC: Definitely. And definitely compared to last year, because it means €95,000 more revenue and almost €95,000 more profit. So a flow-through of almost 100 percent. More questions about Rooms . . . no? Then on to the F&B department: Etienne, can you comment on revenue?

FBM: €172,000 in total revenue; unfortunately we did not make budget; we were 7% under. The shortfall is from all outlets, Banqueting excepted. Especially breakfast did not perform; we're about €6,500 short, or nine percent. The average spend is €16,50 which is a euro over budget but at a lower occupancy; I assume we had more rooms booked without breakfast, because the Executive Lounge breakfast revenues are part of the 6,500 revenue.

FC: In the end we had a somewhat lower capture ratio of in-house guests having breakfast.

FBM: Definitely. There's a downward trend there. The budgeted capture ratio has gone up, for the past year or so, whereas the actual one goes down and down. We need to monitor this.

REVMAN: Indeed, if I look at the numbers, we are down 150 nights for rates including breakfast.

FBM: Any idea as to why?

REVMAN: No, the supplement for breakfast is €15, so that is an attractive price. Perhaps many people book solely looking at the rate, which is of course lower if breakfast is not included . . . No, I don't have a logical explanation for it.

AFM: We are looking into that for the last 6 months, the booking patterns of rates excluding breakfast.

FC: And how about the Corporate rates this year, without breakfast? There's a few of them, right?

AFM: Indeed, mainly Large Automotive Company . . . but because of the loyalty status of many of those guests, the majority has breakfast included. On top of that we had fewer leisure guests, this month versus last year.

FBM: OK, well, at least let's make sure we're on the ball on this one. All outlets except for Banqueting en Minibar showed an increase from February last year, when Banqueting hosted That Big Corporate Party, you remember, in the Ballroom, so it was really impossible to reach that revenue level again. Next week we start the minibar project to see if our product range is the right one, and if we couldn't create alternative or additional revenues, like something in the lobby. The shortfall of €12,000 in revenue had to be compensated on the cost side. We tried really hard and low and behold: for the very first time: full time equivalents 17.59 actual and 17.59 budget so exactly on budget [receives applause]. Thank you!

EC: To continue in that same vein: we have a food cost of . . .22.12%.

FC: How about an applause for that as well?! [Applause].

EC: Because of my . . .

FBM: Fantastic purchasing skills!

EC: Well, yes, but that was compensated for by the other part.

FBM: Thanks for the heads-up, because indeed: *beverage* costs were slightly higher, but bottom-line – simply because food is a bigger slice than beverage – we saved more than €7,500 in cost of sales. We've also been very cautious in Other Expenses; we spent less on just about all of them than budgeted. We came in about €2,500 under budget; and all in all this boils down to an actual departmental profit of €33,500 vis-à-vis a 37,000 budget. That is still a cool 19.5% versus a budgeted 20%.

FC: There is not too much to say about the Other Revenues. Telecom is a few hundred euros over budget; other revenues are a bit under budget but better than last year February; that includes, amongst others, Guest Laundry. We had a very high target of €9,500 for Parking; actual revenue was 8,500, so a bit less, but in absolute terms still very high.

RDM: And in a short time frame, I guess? The typical IAE guests does not get here by car, same for the LMC guest . . .

FC: Yes indeed, about €8,500 on our other guests. Quite happy with that. Rentals and Other Income was quite on budget overall, but that's the effect of two things. Every month we budget a cancellation revenue not knowing if guests will actually cancel and – if the rate booked calls for that – have to pay us. Last month that did not happen. On the other hand we were allowed to invoice the IAE, or rather the venue of IAE, for security we had to arrange for some of the athletes. We of course also have the expense for that, so that will end up in Rentals and Other Income. The two cancel out: it looks as if we are exactly on budget, and we are, but the way in which we achieved that was a bit different from what you'd expect. So you also see a higher cost of sales in Rentals and Other Income, because those revenues were generated a bit differently. Because the invoice we sent to the IAE venue, for security, is actually the invoice we received ourselves, for security. Let's move on to the overhead departments. First A&G. Pretty much all overhead departments have Payroll reasonably in line with budget. A&G was €1,000 over budget. Total expenses here €8,500 over budget and 8,500 more than last year. This is mostly because of the invoice we received for extra security services during the IAE which as we just discussed was booked in A&G; this was €4,500. Then we also spend €2,000 *more* on credit card commission, never mind our slightly *lower* revenue, but that's because our share of American Express was very high: 30.2% of total credit card payments which is more than we're used to. On top of that, 73.6% of all payments were credit cards, which is also higher than we're used to.

GM: That is a very high percentage.

FC: Yes. You'd expect, with these big events and conferences, the percentage credit card payments to be lower; the IAE is of course invoiced . . . but anyway, it was 73.6%. On to Sales and Marketing.

SALES AND MARKETING MANAGER (SM): In Sales and Marketing expenses we were a bit over budget, which can be explained by the transfer of some hours from F&B for the IAE, but other expenses are below budget. Large items, as you know, include Promotion & Entertainment in which all IAE expenses were booked. We saved 2K on a total budget of €50,000, so that helps. Next to that we had a photo shoot which we over-budgeted and managed to spend €750 less. E-commerce was somewhat higher, because of an annual invoice which was budgeted in its entirety for January, but we decided to book as an expense each month, pro rata. But all in all . . . expense-wise a good month for us.

FC: Thank you. Next up is Property Operations.

RDM: Here Payroll is below budget in as far as controllable expenses are concerned, we bought in new uniforms for our engineer, and received some invoices for electronic equipment, including a new lock for the Executive Lounge.

FC: Fine, thanks. Total GOP for the hotel is thus €218,000 versus a budget of €221,000. In other words, as I said before, we only lost €3,000 of GOP with a decrease in revenue of 22,000, which means all of the items we just discussed accounted for a good flow-through on negative revenue: 85%

whereas the target for negative revenue is 35 percent, so we can say we were in control. Also compared to last year we're doing fine: €89,000 more revenue, and €64,000 of that flows through to GOP. So, a 72% flow-through, where the target is normally 65%. But, of course, this depends on the sales mix. If your additional revenue is 100% from Rooms, and 100% the effect of higher ADR, then of course flow-through will go through the roof; if it is purely F&B then we'd expect much lower flow-through. And 72% is a very good flow-through in comparison to a similar month the year before. Let's conclude with a look ahead to the next two months. Would you care to enlighten us about the March and April forecasts, Igor?

REVMAN: Sure, first the March forecast. I slightly lowered the Rooms revenues for the Group segment. Group Leisure, that is tours, they're not going well, not just with us, but city-wide. I decreased it by 100 nights. Transient on the other hand is performing, so the total forecast is 880 nights, including [airline] Crew, and Transient Rooms is at 3,700, so we'll make budget. For March we are forecasting an ADR of €133.38 – budget is €131.35. April will be a busy month, we are going to reach budget for sure, and mainly because of groups, conferences and another International Athletic Event. The latter weekend is going to be very strong, ADR will hit €223 euro and the shoulder dates are also selling well. Two hotels have been completely bought out for four days, so we benefit from that quite a bit. And the last week is spring break and sees a large conference in the International Conference Centre which is known to get us big group bookings.

FC: A hundred grand over budget?

REVMAN: Well, let's see where we stand right now . . . I am comparing current pickup and that of last year . . . ADR for the month is already €145, budget was €138.

FC: A great month to look forward to.

GM: A good month to do some renovations! [people laughing]

FC: Let's agree on the following. By the end of March, when we'll have a better idea of the actual revenue for April, then I'd like to look at which departments expect expenses related to our renovation. Perhaps everyone would agree to send me, by then, their take on what impact they expect on for example housekeeping, that's the first one that crosses my mind. But also, on extra payroll for moving furniture about, and relocating the breakfast room.

GM: It is indeed a good suggestion to communicate the increase in revenue to the owner, but to make sure their expectations in terms of GOP stay realistic.

FC: You mean there won't be a 100% flow-through of the additional revenues. Good. Does anyone have any questions about the results? No? Then we close the meeting.

Note

1 Figure 1.1 is not, strictly speaking, *the* USALI income statement format. USALI has owner and operator versions of the "Summary Operating Statements", and more detailed (sub) schedules. Figure 1.1 is an attempt to pull together structural elements from these different formats, in order to provide students with a one-figure overview of the USALI system.

CHAPTER

2 Balance sheet and ratios

Learning outcomes

At the end of this chapter, readers should:

- be able to explain the differences and the relationship between the balance sheet and the income statement;
- identify and describe the main categories of items on a balance sheet;
- appreciate the meaning, relevance and shortcomings of (the numbers presented on a) balance sheet;
- understand the concept of financial ratios and be able to use them in financial analysis.

THEORY

Rob van Ginneken

Introduction

We have already encountered the two financial perspectives in Chapter 1. On an income statement, as you remember, are the revenues and expenses a company incurs in doing business. In the current chapter, we will discuss the second perspective, focussing on what an organisation owns and owes. Just to get some of the accounting jargon out of the way: things that you can own and that have a monetary value, are called "assets". If you owe someone money, or other assets, or even owe them a service such as hospitality, we call this a "liability". Assets and liabilities are reported on the financial statement called balance sheet. You may not come across this statement again – after your Accounting exams, that is – in the very first few years of your hospitality career. But having a basic grasp of what it is will definitely make you a better manager. And as the balance sheet is different from, but clearly linked to that all-important income statement, studying it will enhance your understanding of both.

DOI: 10.4324/9781003545903-2

Balance sheet basics

Let's start our exploration of the balance sheet phenomenon by looking at an overview of an imaginary student's assets and liabilities. Sharonna Beach just started college in Nanaimo, on Vancouver Island, Canada. We will put the things she owns, that is the assets, in one column (the left one) and the debts she has, or liabilities, in a column on the right. All amounts are in Canadian dollars.

Please note that the overview has a date. We are reporting Sharonna's assets and liabilities as they are *today*. Today she has a bike, which we value at $50, and today she owes the bank $150 for the study loan she started taking out. It really doesn't matter when she has to pay back the money. This may not be until after graduation, but there is no question she *does* owe the money, so we put it in the overview.

This simple overview raises some interesting questions. One such question: how do we come up with a value for the bike? Maybe Sharonna remembers what she paid for the bike a few years ago, and took off some of the value. In other words: using depreciation, she arrived at a value today of $50. Another way to get to a value to put in the overview (we call this the book value of the asset) is that she could guess for what the market value would be: what amount would she be able to sell it for, today?

Another question could be: does anyone owe Sharonna any money? Maybe Sharonna went out last night with some fellow students and one of them borrowed some money from her. Or she worked for a temp agency last summer and some of her wages still have to be paid out. If so, this would be an asset (something of value) for her, because in a sense you then "own" something: a claim to somebody else's assets. Another way of looking at this: the money is hers, it's just that it is still in somebody else's pockets at the moment.

What she OWNs (assets)		What she OWES (liabilities)	
Bike	50		
Cell phone	400		
		Study loan	150
Bank account	240		
Cash	10		
Total	700	*Total*	150

Figure 2.1 Overview of assets and liabilities for Sharonna Beach, 12 September 2025

There is, of course, a name for this kind of overview. We call it a balance sheet. Or – many accounting phenomena go by two different names – a "statement of financial position". People that are (or think they are) more fluent than you are in accounting, will tell you the balance sheet should always balance. What they mean is that the total amount on the left should be equal to the total on the right. Our overview does not balance: Sharonna owns more than she owes. Luckily, we can easily balance the balance sheet by adding the difference between the total asset value and the total liabilities to the right-hand side of the overview. In fact, doing so will make it a real balance sheet.

Balance sheet Sharonna Beach, 12/9/2025

What she OWNs (assets)		What she OWES (liabilities) and equity	
Bike	50	Equity	550
Cell phone	400		
		Study loan	150
Bank account	240		
Cash	10		
Total	700	*Total*	700

Figure 2.2 Overview of assets, liabilities and equity for Sharonna Beach, 12 September 2025

We call this the (owner's) equity. The value of $550 means the value of Sharonna's assets exceeds that of her liabilities by $550. Some people call equity "net worth" and that illustrates nicely what it is: it is a measure of how rich Sharonna is. The value of everything she owns may be $700, but if, at the same time, she also has a debt of $150, you could say she's really worth only $550. All of this is often referred as "the balance sheet equation": total assets = total liabilities + owner's equity.

Now, most individuals don't make balance sheets – although for some it would not be a bad idea. All organisations, on the other hand, do. Here's a simple example of the items an organisation's balance sheet could contain.

You may have noticed this balance sheet is ordered a bit differently, along the vertical direction, from Sharonna's. The order on the left is from what are called *current* assets – assets the business is likely to use, or convert to cash within a year – to what are called *fixed* or *non-current* assets, which are going to be used for more than a year. On the right-hand side, we have short-term liabilities (these are going to be paid within the next 12 months) on top, followed by long-term loans such as the mortgage here. Last is the owner's equity. Both ways of ordering the balance sheet are OK, as long as you are

Balance sheet ACME, Inc. 12/31/2025

Assets		Liabilities and owner's equity	
Current assets		*Short-term liabilities*	
Cash	1,000	Accounts payable	50,000
Bank	9,000		
Inventory	30,000	*Long-term liabilities*	
Accounts receivable	20,000	Mortgage loan	950,000
Fixed assets		*Owner's equity*	
Building	2,000,000	Common stock	500,000
Furniture	440,000	Retained earnings	1,000,000
Total	2,500,000	Total	2,500,000

Figure 2.3 Balance sheet for ACME Inc., 31 December 2025

consistent. From current to non-current assets on the left? Then also from short-term liabilities to long-term liabilities to equity at the right.

Also, there are a few new names on this balance sheet. We can't discuss all possible balance sheet items in this chapter, but the ones in this sample are on most companies' statements and you ought to be familiar with them. "Inventory" is the value of the goods the business is selling. For a hospitality operation, that would come down to food and beverage, or bathrobes if the hotel is selling them, or golf paraphernalia for the golf pro shop, or skin treatments in the spa. They are on the balance sheet at cost, so valued at what the business paid for them, not at the selling price. "Accounts receivable" refers to amounts owed to the business by its guests – unpaid bills, that is. Depending on the nature of the business, "A/R", as it is often abbreviated, may or may not be a significant sum. The restaurant business is mostly cash sales, but then again: every now and then guests will expect to be billed, e.g. for an event the restaurant catered. Or credit card companies may take their time paying the business the amounts charged by guests to their credit card. On the other hand, guests may also pay (part of) what they owe in advance. This "advance deposits", as it is called in accounting, would be *where* on a balance sheet, you guess? Let's say the guest transfers the money of the advance payment to the bank account of the restaurant; that would increase the latter's "bank" balance on the left-hand side of the balance sheet. But (remember the recognition principle from Chapter 1?) the money is not really the restaurant's: they have not done anything for it, yet. So, they also record the money as an "advance deposit" in the short-term liabilities part of the balance sheet, almost as a note to self: "We still owe this guest some hospitality". By now you surely understand that the "accounts payable", or "A/P" item on the balance sheet is the amount of money owed by the business to its suppliers for items delivered but not yet paid.

The mortgage loan on our sample balance sheet is just one of many different kinds of long-term debt. This type specifically is used to finance land and buildings and as such, will be on the balance sheet of hospitality businesses which own the real estate they operate in.

In the owner's equity section of this sample we see two items – again, there may be more but that's the stuff more advanced finance texts are made of. Common stock, or common shares, represents the original investment of the owners (shareholders/stockholders) of the business. "Retained earnings" is the total amount of profits not paid out to the owners. This probably requires a bit of explanation. Let's say your resort's golf pro shop sells a set of balls for $25, which they bought for $10. Ignoring, for simplicity's sake, all other expenses involved, the shop makes a profit of $15. How would the balance sheet change as a result of this transaction? The Accounting employee would decrease the number for "inventory" by $10 – remember inventory is recorded at cost. Then, she would increase "cash" (if the guest is paying cash), "bank" (if he is using his debit card), or "accounts receivable" (if the guest insists on being billed) by $25. Good for the shop, but the downside is that the balance sheet now no longer balances. Actually, it does, because the third and last entry the Accounting employee will make in the accounting system is to increase "retained earnings" by $15. A *decrease* in retained earnings occurs when the owners decide to take some of the accumulated profits out of the firm (the current asset "bank" decreases, and by taking the money out of the business, the value of that business will also decrease). The company may also have a loss instead of a profit in a given accounting period. That loss would also be subtracted from retained earnings. It is possible to incur such heavy or recurring losses that retained earnings would eventually become negative and even total equity would be negative.

What does a balance sheet really tell us?

Keeping track of, and knowing at all times the value of, one's assets and liabilities is an important issue in the world of finance. On the operating level, a business will need to adjust the value of goods in inventory in case some items have disappeared because of theft or waste. On the "corporate finance" level, the shareholders may want to study the balance sheet to determine if the value for Owner's Equity merits the paying out of dividends – and, just as importantly: whether there is enough money in the business's bank accounts to do so!

A quick recap. You should know by now that:

- the income statement is the report that measures how much value was generated in each accounting period;
- the balance sheet lists the values of what the business owns and owes, to its creditors and shareholders, at a certain moment in time.

To further enhance your understanding of the exact nature of the statements, let's discuss if and how these statements can help us value the business as a whole. "Wait a minute!" I hear some of you say: "Didn't you just say (in the Sharonna example) that equity represented the value of a person or business?" Well, yes and no. Let's explore.

Say Sharonna loves French fries and her deepest desire is to one day own a fries shop. And low and behold, the owner of The French Friar[1] in Nanaimo is ready to retire and has put his shop on the market! How much should Sharonna expect to pay for it, lock, stock and barrel – meaning she would buy the entire company, so not just the building or any of the other assets?

Some details that you may consider to be of interest:

- The French Friar is located in a popular part of downtown Nanaimo;
- the owner is known by all as Fred and is a very friendly man of Belgian descent;
- Fred serves the best French fries on Vancouver Island.

What else would you want to know about The French Friar to be able to make a bid for the place? When we discuss this case in my lectures, most students at this time indicate they want to know the value of the building. Let's just say it is $400,000. What then? You can go on along these lines, asking for the value of the frying installation, the inventory of fries and other foods and beverages, the cash in cash registers and bank accounts, and so on. It sure makes sense that the value of the company would somehow be based on the value of its assets. But as you can hopefully imagine, the value of the building, which will probably be the highest-value asset, is not necessarily a good indication of the value of the company. The building is in a rather up-scale residential neighborhood, so real estate is expensive, but what if the people here don't like French fries, and there are no tourists? So, it makes sense to focus on another aspect of the fries shop: how much business is it doing? In other words: how much value is this building generating for the owner?

Revenue would be a good indication that there actually is a market for the company's products. Profit may be an even better indication, because this also tells you how efficiently the current owner has managed the operation.

Remember, profit is the difference between revenue and expenses, in other words how much of the revenue is left after all expenses have been taken into account. If Sharonna already has plans to completely reorganize after taking over from Fred, the latter's profit may not be as relevant, and Sharonna should focus on revenue as the relevant basis for determining a price. Of course, she should not simply ask Fred how much profit he made last year. Maybe this was an exceptionally good or bad year. Much better would be to ask for the shop's income statements and balance sheets for the last three, or even five years. Doing an in-depth investigation of the target business is standard procedure in the case of companies taking over, or merging with, other companies. It is called "due diligence" and meant to get a good insight into the financial situation of the target company. The buying party wants to rule out any possible "skeletons in the closet". In real life, you would use simple rules of thumb to get from profit or revenue to a purchase price. A simple example would be to use a multiplier and offer to buy the company for seven times profit. Or two or three times revenue.

So, at first glance, the value of a firm's assets is not necessarily a good indication of the true value of the company. But what if we are looking at the current owner's "books" anyway, in our due diligence efforts, and we have access to not only the income statement, but also the balance sheet? Is it really and completely useless?

Could we use this information to arrive at a figure for the value of the company? As noted before, the value of the assets, as represented on the balance sheet, may not be the same as the value these assets create in terms of (future) profit. But there is another reason that you can't simply say the balance sheet total is the same as the value of the firm. The reason is in the liabilities. Basically, $355,000 worth of assets is not owned by the company, but rather by its creditors. That is, the company legally owns the assets but has to keep in mind that it has essentially locked up other people's money in these assets.

Balance Sheet 'The French Friar', 31 December 2025

Assets		Liabilities and owner's equity	
Total current assets	550		
FF&E	1,000	Total current and long-term liabilities	355,000
Building	400,000		
		Owner's equity	46,550
Total	$ 401,550	Total	$ 401,550

Figure 2.4 Balance sheet for "The French Friar", 31 December 2025

Should the company decide to sell all of the assets and use the money proceeds to pay off the debts, it would have $46,550 left. This represents the value of the company to the owner, and we call this "net worth", "net asset value" or, as we have called it in this balance sheet, "owner's equity".

So here we have an indication of the value, again. Would you pay $46,550 for the fries shop? Do you think Fred would be willing to sell it to you for that amount? Personally, I don't think so. The reason is the one discussed before: included in Owner's Equity is the book value of the assets, which is not necessarily the real (market) value of the assets. But this real value, based on The French Friar's reputation for excellence, its prime location, its loyal fries-loving clientele . . . is not on the balance sheet! Why not? The reputation of The French Friar is an example of an intangible fixed asset (IFA). There are basically two reasons why you won't find these on a balance sheet.

- It is difficult to put an exact number on "things" like reputation. More difficult than for a tangible fixed asset, anyway;
- Even if you have come to what you think is the right value: how sure can you be of it? To give an example: how sure can you be that your super-motivated and well-trained staff will actually stay with you? How sure can you be that this great patent you have on this cool invention, will not, tomorrow, be suddenly be made obsolete (and thus: worthless) by an even better invention by one of your competitors? Think of taxi drivers that paid huge sums of money to get a taxi permit, just before the advent of Uber.

There is one major exception to the rule just mentioned, and that's after a take-over. How does this work? Assume Sharonna comes to an agreement with Fred and buys The French Friar for $200,000. That means she paid $153,450 in excess of owner's equity. This must mean that she thinks the reputation – and other possible intangibles that are not on the balance sheet – have a joint value of $153,450. If she indeed paid this premium over owner's equity, the value of the IFAs of The French Friar has now "materialized", simply because "the market" has now put a price on them: $153,450. This means that if Sharonna actually closes the deal and buys The French Friar, she can put this value on the balance sheet. She would label it "goodwill" – because that's the name it goes by in Finance and Accounting.

Of course this triggers a further question: now what? You already know most fixed assets are written off over their useful life, that is, the purchase price is spread out over the period you expect it to produce financial benefits for your organisation. Do we also do this with IFAs? The answer is: it depends. If you have an IFA with a definite useful life (e.g. a patent that is awarded to you for a certain number of years) you do. Whereas we use the word depreciation for writing off tangible fixed assets, for IFAs we use the word amortization. Only the word is different, what we actually do is the same:

- determine the useful life;
- decide how much we are going to write off (all of the value or just part of it, if we assume a certain residual value at the end of the asset's useful life);
- choose a method, such as straight-line, for writing off.

For IFAs with an *in*definite life (goodwill is a good example: you don't know how long you are going to profit from the good reputation The French Friar had under Fred's rule), it works a bit differently. Discussion of this last topic is outside the scope of this Essentials book and may be covered in a more advanced textbook. If curious, ask your lecturer for the meaning of "impairment".

Ratios and benchmarking

Plenty more could be said about balance sheets. But the statement *itself* is not too interesting, probably, to hospitality managers. It really is about how to give meaning to the items and amounts on the balance sheet, or for that matter, any financial report. In Chapter 1 we showed how expressing certain line items as a percentage of the bigger whole (revenue, in the case of an income statement) may provide extra meaning. The same goes for balance sheet items: knowing what percentage of a business' assets is current, or what percentage of assets is financed by long-term debt, may be of use to management.

Ratio analysis includes and goes beyond expressing numbers as a percentage of another number. It also goes beyond just comparing numbers from either the income statement or the balance sheet. Some ratios divide a number from the income statement by another number from the balance sheet. You might think: but aren't we then comparing apples and oranges? Didn't these two statements represent two different financial perspectives? They do indeed, and that's exactly why it is sometimes useful, even for management of operating departments, to study a number from one of the statements in the light of a number from the other.

Before we go on to discuss the most important (groups of) ratios, it is important to mention that different company stakeholders are interested in different aspects of the business. Lenders and other creditors such as suppliers – or employees, for that matter – will be interested in whether the business will be able to pay them what they are owed. Shareholders have a different focus; they want to know whether the business will generate healthy and growing levels of profit for every dollar invested. Managers are interested in ratios that help them manage staffing levels, track performance vis-à-vis their comp set, or keep purchasing expenses in check. Sometimes these different stakeholders also evaluate the same ratios differently: what is good for one stakeholder may not be acceptable to another. We'll see an example of that shortly.

All accounting books will present ratios (there's easily tens, and perhaps even hundreds of them) in groups. The number of groups, their names and the ratios included in each group may differ from one book to the next, so please don't get too hung up on that. Here's our concise version, in just four groups.

Liquidity ratios

The first group of ratios is typically called liquidity ratios. These convey information about whether a business will be able to meet all its short-term financial obligations. In other words: will it be able to pay this month's salaries, make next month's debt service, and so on. One easy way to answer that question is to look at the total for short-term liabilities and see how much current assets are available. The idea is that current assets are either cash or will be converted into cash shortly, so the total could be used to pay whatever needs to be paid. Say total current assets are $50,000 at a certain date, and short-term liabilities $40,000. Possibly the most famous ratio of all, the so-called current ratio divides the former by the latter to give us 1.25. If this ratio exceeds 1, that is if current assets outnumber short-term liabilities, that is considered a good thing.

You may have observed a weakness of this ratio: some inventory may not be sold and converted into cash soon; some guests may be slow to pay your "accounts receivable", while some large short-term liabilities may be due tomorrow rather than in a few months' time. For that reason, many companies would prefer for their current ratio to be 1.5 or even 2 rather than 1. Maybe we should be more specific and say that *management* would prefer higher values for this ratio. The *owners* of the business might frown on high levels of inventory, accounts receivable and cash, and consider their investment poorly managed.

Other liquidity ratios are the quick ratio (where the inventories are left out of the equation for the reason mentioned above), or net working capital, which is current assets less (rather than divided by) short-term liabilities.

Solvency ratios

A second and related group of ratios looks at all of the business' financial obligations, not just the short-term ones. Businesses calculate two types of ratios to determine whether they are solvent, that is if it is likely they can meet all of their obligations. The first type looks at the composition of items on the right-hand side of the balance sheet: how much debt is used to finance the business? The more debt, the more challenging it is to make all associated debt service payments, all other things equal. There are many different ways to express the extent to which debt rather than equity is used:

- total debt, or sometimes only total *long-term* debt, as a percentage of total assets: TD / TA × 100%;

- total assets divided by total debt: TA / TD;
- owner's equity as a percentage of total assets: OE / TA × 100%;
- total debt divided by owner's equity: TD / OE: this is known as the debt-to-equity ratio.

Be careful in interpreting solvency ratios: depending on which one is used, either a high *or* a low value represents good solvency. A high debt to equity ratio means low solvency, but a high value for TA/TD means high solvency. When is solvency high enough? It is generally accepted for a firm to have more debt than equity – so a debt-to-equity ratio of more than 1 – but not much more. At a debt-to-equity ratio of 3, for example, 75% of a business' assets are financed by lenders and just 25% by the owners. At such a low level of solvency, lenders may become a bit nervous that in case of a bankruptcy they may not get all of their money back. If you don't monitor your solvency, rest assured your bank does!

The second type of ratios looks not just at the amount of debt, but also at the levels of cash flow generated by the business. The latter is of course what will be used to service that debt: to make repayments and pay interest. Banks may refuse to lend money to a firm with a "total debt to EBITDA" ratio of more than 5, in other words a firm that already has borrowed more than 5 times what they generate in terms of EBITDA per year. Here you see a first example of a ratio combining a number from the balance sheet with one from the income statement. Hopefully you also see how this makes sense. A second example of such a ratio is the "debt service coverage ratio" (DSCR): here the cash flow generated in a period is divided by the debt service payments to be made in that same period. Please consider again the different interpretations: a high "total debt to EBITDA" ratio means low solvency, whereas a high DSCR means high solvency.

Profitability ratios

As important as the ratios just discussed are, chances are you will be exposed to quite others in the first years of your career. Net profit margin was already discussed in Chapter 1. Another margin-type ratio is the GOP percentage (gross operating profit as a percentage of revenue) closely monitored by most hotels. For restaurants, the gross profit margin (revenue less cost of sales as a percentage of revenues) is one of the key metrics; much more about this in the "Finance and Accounting in F&B" chapter.

Investors want to know how the value of their investment is developing. If you consider that net profit is the value generated by a firm for its owners, expressing that as a percentage of their investment gives them their return on every dollar invested. "Return on Equity" = net profit in a year / average owner's equity × 100%. To calculate the average, add the value of equity at the beginning and end of the year and divide by two. "Earnings per share" is net profit divided by the total number of shares and another way for an owner to gauge the profitability of their investment.

Operating ratios

This group contains more ratios than any other, especially in our case since many hospitality-specific ratios are in it. ADR (average daily rate), occupancy percentage and RevPAR (revenue per available room) are arguably the three key operating ratios for hotels. You may already be familiar with them from an introductory course in hotel management, but just in case you are not: a small example of how these are calculated. A very small boutique hotel has ten rooms. On a given night, seven are sold. Three rooms for $150, and the remaining four rooms for $175 each.

- occupancy: 7 / 10 × 100% = 70%;
- ADR is the average rate of the rooms sold: (3 × $150 + 4 × $175) / 7 = $1.150 / 7 = $164.29;
- RevPAR is $1,150 / 10 = $115.

Please note that RevPAR is a combination of occupancy and ADR: 70% of $164.29 is $115. Occupancy and ADR in separation only paint part of the performance picture. It is easy to achieve high occupancy: advertising low rates will do the trick. It may also be easy to achieve high ADRs, assuming there is always someone willing to pay top dollar – or as it is called in the hotel business: rack rate. But generating high average rates at equally high levels of occupancy: that is the real challenge! This important discipline in our industry is called "Revenue Management".

Other typical hospitality examples include "seat turnover" (number of diners in a shift/number of seats), and "average check" (food and beverage revenue/number of covers) for a restaurant. More generic ratios used in the industry are the so-called "turnover" ratios. These measure the speed with which certain assets are converted into cash. Consider the following example, of the inventory turnover ratio: annual cost of sales/average level of inventory.

Assuming yearly cost of sales of $250,000 and an average inventory level of $25,000, would give us an inventory turnover of ten times: the business sells their inventory ten times per year. Turnover ratios are often expressed in a way that is perhaps easier to understand: as a "number of days". In this case, "ten times" a year is equivalent to 365 (days in a year) / 10, an average of 36.5 days an item spends in inventory. If this happens to be the inventory of a watch shop specializing in expensive dress watches, this would be quite acceptable. For a bakery, definitely not!

Conclusion

Perhaps you found this chapter a bit less interesting than the one before. Admittedly, a balance sheet is a bit more conceptual in nature, more "haute finance" you might say, than an income statement. And as such it may often be more interesting for accountants and bookkeepers, for investors and banks than for managers. But as said in the Introduction, having a basic understanding of what a balance sheet is, as well as its limitations, will expand your financial horizon. This in turn will mean you can engage in more meaningful (ratio) analysis and thus enable you to make better decisions. May the following practice section serve as a small teaser.

PRACTICE: PIECING THE PUZZLE

Agatha Engel

On the bus home from school you find a bunch of papers on the seat next to you. They appear to be the balance sheet and income statement of a certain organisation.[2] The statements do not mention what company it is, what industry it is in, or if it is performing well. Let's refer to it as "Mystery Company", or MC from now. You, being the smart student you are, decide to analyse the financial statements and this is what you find.

The first lines of the income statement state two types of revenue:

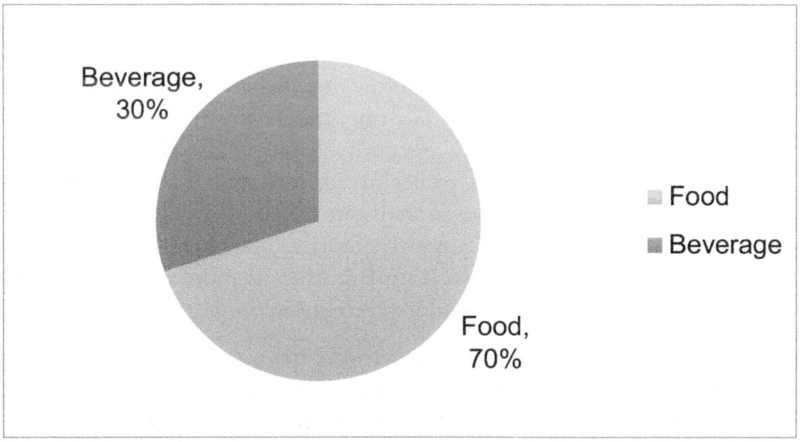

Figure 2.5 Sales mix for MC

OK, so this must be some kind of restaurant serving food (70%) and beverages (30%). From your Accounting classes you remember that the cost of sales percentage could tell you something about the type of restaurant: is it fast food like McDonald's, fresh casual like Vapiano, or perhaps a fancy restaurant?

Table 2.1 Cost of sales percentage for the year 2017

	McDonald's (fast food)	*Vapiano (fresh casual)*	*MC*
Cost of sales food	31.7%	25.05%	38%

Let's find out how much the cost of sales is of each of these companies. For McDonald's, looking at the 2017 figures (McDonald's Annual Report, 2017), the cost of sales percentage is calculated as cost of food US$4,033.5 million divided by US$12,718.9 million revenue from owned[3] restaurants, which makes 31.7%. For Vapiano (Vapiano Annual Report, 2017), the cost of sales percentage is 25.05%, calculated as calculated cost of food €81,360 thousand divided by revenue of €324,699 thousand. For MC the cost of sales percentage is 38%, calculated as food cost 225,000 divided by 600,000 food revenue.

MC seems to have a very high cost of sales percentage compared to the other two companies. There could be an explanation for this, for example a certain business model that is built around a high cost of sales. Just from the cost of sales percentage you can't be certain if that is indeed the case, or whether MC is perhaps having trouble managing their food costs. Having a restaurant means you will always have cost of sales. This means that running a restaurant is not about eliminating cost of sales, but managing these costs. If you are competing against fast food restaurants you don't want to have a higher percentage than your direct competition. How much that cost of sales percentage is, depends on a number of factors. For one, the type of restaurant; fast food, fresh casual, or more formal dining. Secondly, location also plays an important role; sales prices and ingredient prices are different in Switzerland than in Romania. For a Big Mac you have to shell out US$6.54 in Switzerland, versus a mere US$2.32 in Romania (Economist/Statista, 2018). But from the sales price alone you can't deduce that selling Big Macs is more profitable in Switzerland than in Romania. You would need to know the ingredient cost as well.

Comparing cost of sales percentage only works in your direct comp set. If you want to compare more generally you will want to compare "margin", i.e. how much do you have left after cost of sales? Technically, margin is gross profit (sales minus cost of sales) as a percentage of sales. Margin is used to pay for all other expenses not being cost of sales, for example payroll and admin.

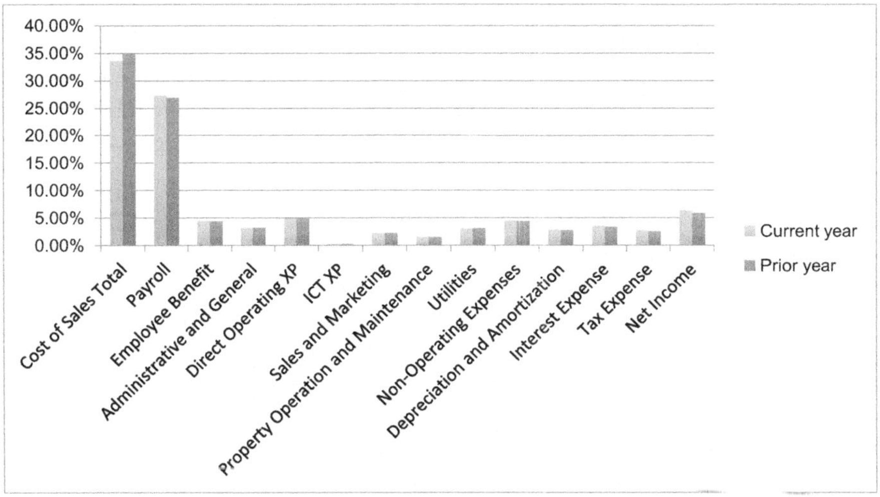

Figure 2.6 Common-size income statement for MC

So, what other costs does MC have, and how big are they in comparison to their sales? You decide to create a full overview of the income statement, and express each item as a percentage of revenue. Figure 2.6 is the graph you create for the current and prior year. The first thing you notice is that the second biggest cost for MC is payroll (labour costs and related expenses). This is to be expected if you are running a restaurant. Even fast food restaurants still have people working the grill and fryer. In the future this percentage may change when technology, ordering kiosks and apps replace personnel (Johnson, 2018).

Comparing MC to McDonald's and Vapiano, you find the following payroll cost percentages for the year 2017

Table 2.2 Payroll as a percentage of revenue, 2017

	McDonald's (fast food)	*Vapiano (fresh casual)*	*MC*
Payroll	27.7%	42.06%	27%

The payroll percentage is not helping you decide whether MC looks more like McDonald's or like Vapiano. You decide to do a bit of reasoning to imagine what it would look like in terms of seats and customers.

The average food check is €4.18 (US$4.72) for McDonald's (Lutz, 2015). For MC, this would translate into 600,000 of food revenue / 4.18 average food check / 365 days = 393 customers a day. If they actually had three seatings with no seat turnover, this would be 393 / 3 = 131 customers per seating. On the other hand, using the average food check of €11 of Vapiano (Vapiano Investor Information, 2017), food revenue 600,000 / 11 average food check / 365 days = 149 customers a day. If there are three seatings, this translates into roughly 49 customers per seating.

Up till now you have used the cost of sales and payroll cost of MC working on the assumption they have been recorded correctly. In order to check if they have, you cross check with the balance sheet accounts inventory and payroll payable. If some of the costs were not recorded correctly or fully you would expect a sudden change in inventory or payroll payable on the balance sheet. Inventory decreased by 7% but this seems to be in line with a 6% decrease in sales. Selling less means purchasing less. When you look at payroll payable, there is not even a 1% change in the balance sheet account. The payroll cost as a percentage of revenue does not change either. Both balance sheet accounts seem to be recorded correctly. However, it could be that cost of sales is extraordinarily high because it is not managed efficiently. In order to determine this, you calculate two ratios called "days inventory" and "inventory turnover". Days inventory, calculated as average inventory divided by daily cost of sales, tells us how long on average inventory spends in storage before being sold. It turns out to be 18,5 days. Translating this number to inventory turnover, 365 divided by days inventory (365 / 18.5= 19.7) gets you roughly twenty times a year that the inventory is filled and emptied. When compared to the industry (category food and drinking places, Wilson, 2017) that has a turnover over 30, it is clear that inventory is not managed very well.

You wonder if inventory is the only problem and compare the accounts receivable turnover and asset turnover of MC with the industry. Where MC has an accounts receivable turnover of ten times a year, the industry turns their accounts receivable over 162 times a year. While it is true that collecting money from your guests will take longer if you cater to specific segments, for example business as opposed to consumers, MC is waiting more than a month for its customers to pay them. (365 / turnover of 10.21 = 35.7 days accounts collection)

The same problem appears when managing assets, where MC is turning the assets over once per year, the industry has a triple asset turnover. This means that the industry is able to get more revenue out of their assets. So what assets does MC actually have? You decide to look at the balance sheet, and start at a high level. How many current versus non-current assets do they have? The majority turns out to be non-current assets (87%). Most of the non-current assets are the building and the land. You would like to know if the high proportion of non-current assets is normal.

Initially, you wanted to compare McDonald's and Vapiano but you remember that these companies are chain companies that franchise brand names and

Table 2.3 Comparing turnover ratio for MC with industry benchmark

	MC	*Industry* (Wilson, 2017)
Inventory turnover	19.7	30.8
Accounts receivable turnover	10.21	162.5
Asset turnover	1.11	3.3

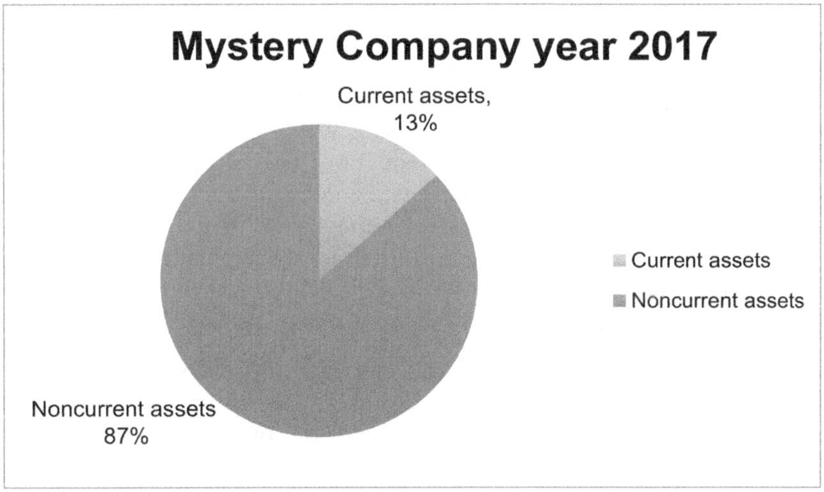

Figure 2.7 Asset composition MC, 2017

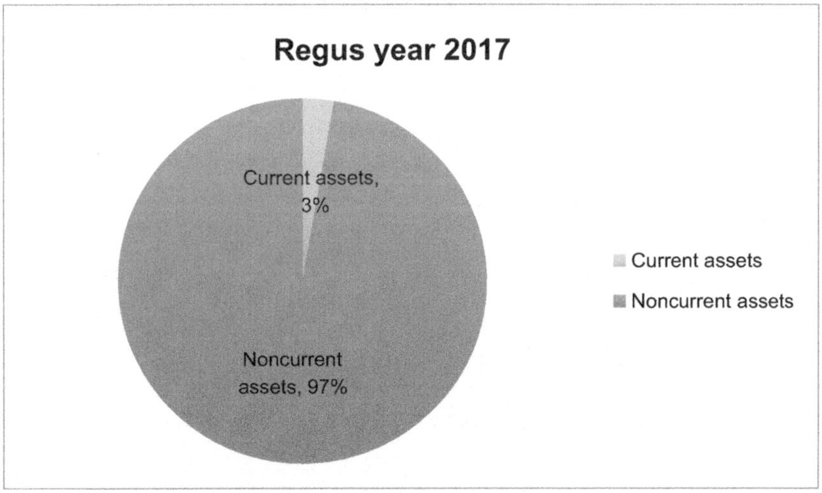

Figure 2.8 Asset composition Regus, 2017

recipes. This means that many assets will be owned by the franchise-taker (the "franchisee") and not by the company that bears the name (the "franchisor"). Hmm, so what company could you compare MC to? You are trying to come up with extremely asset-heavy companies. One company comes to mind: Regus, a company that rents out office space in buildings it owns. It turns out Regus (Annual Report, 2017) has 97% in non-current assets. This is what you expected.

You decide to look up another likely asset heavy company, what about an airline, such as Singapore Airlines (Annual Report, 2017). You find that Singapore Airlines has 82% in non-current assets. Singapore Airlines owns (as of March 2018) 122 aircrafts, and in addition it leases 69 aircrafts. That's interesting: MC has more non-current assets (percentage wise) than an airliner! Hmm, so companies make different choices. While you need certain assets to operate your business, office space to rent it out, and airplanes to fly them, it is not always necessary to own the assets. Some companies choose to go a bit "asset-lighter" and lease (that is rent) the assets. The choice is reflected in the Income Statement. If you own the building you will see depreciation expense and probably some interest expense, if you financed the purchase through a loan. On the other hand, if you lease the assets, you will have the rent expense.

Knowing that MC owns the building and the land has shifted your focus to their financing (Table 2.4). Did they use solely equity or maybe a mix of equity and debt to finance the purchase of the building and the land? It turns out that MC has an almost 50/50 split between debt and equity. An

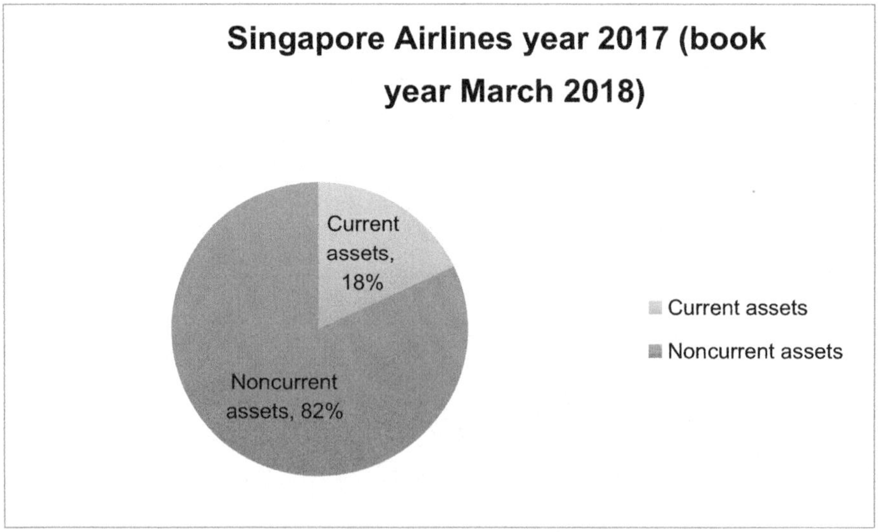

Figure 2.9 Asset composition Singapore Airlines, 2017

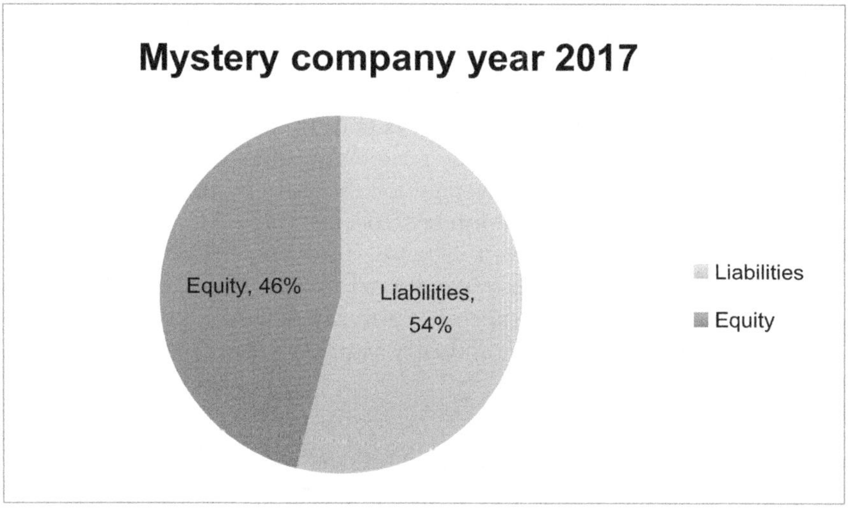

Figure 2.10 Debt to equity, MC, 2017

equal split sounds safe, similar to everyday life scenarios where you split the cost between yourself and a friend of yours, but does this 50/50 rule work in finance? Is it possible to have 80% debt and only 20% equity?

When comparing to your industry benchmark (Wilson, 2017) you find that the industry average is 75% debt, and 25% equity. In other words, most of MC's competitors chose a different ratio of debt to equity. But why would a company want to have more debt, i.e. be more financially leveraged? Using the return on equity (ROE) ratio to explain this rationale, you see that even if companies start with similar profit margins (roughly 6%) the proportion of debt determines how much of the profit ends up with the owners (equity): 15% for MC, versus a whopping 77% for the industry! In other words, for each euro the owners have invested, the business generates 15 cents (MC) versus 78 cents for the industry average. From an investor point of view, MC is not very attractive. A way to explain the leverage effect is to imagine profit as a bag of cookies. Sharing a bag of cookies with two others will likely mean you get a decent share of the bag. Sharing that same bag of cookies with 30 others means your share is greatly reduced.

This financial leverage effect would mean that MC would want more debt if banks would give it to them. This in turn makes you wonder how banks look at MC: how risky does the company look to banks? One of the first questions that come to mind is: can MC pay their short-term debts, i.e. what is their current and quick ratio? The current and quick ratios shown in Table 2.5 are not far from the industry average. This means that MC is able to pay their short-term debts, and their ability to pay back is similar to that of the competition. So far, so good for MC.

What about a longer time frame? To evaluate a longer time frame you check if the annual earnings before interest and tax (EBIT) can cover the annual interest expense, i.e. the interest coverage ratio. Wow, here MC is clearly behind the competition! The industry average for the ratio is roughly ten, for MC it is only three. To improve the interest coverage ratio MC could try to get a higher EBIT or a lower interest expense. To increase their EBIT they can increase revenue and or decrease operational expenses like cost of sales and payroll. As for their interest expense, currently MC is paying roughly 3% of revenue in interest while the industry is paying less than 1%, while the industry has more debt!

Table 2.4 Comparing financial leverage of MC with industry benchmark

	MC (%)	*Industry average (%)*
Profit margin (net income / revenue)	6.3	5.9
Debt % (D / E)	54	74.9
ROE (net income / E)	15.30	77.5

Table 2.5 Comparing financial health ratio of MC with industry benchmark

	MC	*Industry average*
Current ratio (CA / CL)	1.33	1.2
Quick ratio (QA / CL)	0.97	0.9
Interest coverage ratio (EBIT / Interest)	3.56	10.3
Debt %	54%	74.9%
Interest expense %	3.5%	0.6%

You have been so caught up in your papers that you missed your bus stop. You decide to get out and grab a bite to eat while you write your thoughts down.

> MC serves food and beverage. Those are their two revenue streams. Their cost of sales seems a bit high in comparison to McDonald's and Vapiano but you don't know MC's business model. You do think that their inventory and accounts receivable could be better managed. In addition, MC chose to own the building and the land and finance half of the non-current assets with debt. The industry average uses more debt, and hence is more financially leveraged.

While writing your thoughts down, you think back to your placement company from last year: Scandic Hotels (Annual Report, 2017). What would you read in the financial statements of a hotel?

First, there would obviously be room revenue and this would make up most of the sales mix. If the hotel is "full service" there could also be food and beverage revenue. You google the financial statements of Scandic (Annual Report, 2017) and find that 60% is indeed room revenue, and about 30% is F&B and conference revenue. This is what you expected. There is a note about the revenue, and when you check it, you see that a large part of the room revenue is from leased hotels. Scandic Hotels is a big company, and only owns a small part of the hotel buildings they operate.

When you scroll down to the expenses you see that the biggest part (roughly 30%) is personnel cost. This makes sense, as there are usually front desk personnel and back office personnel, and maybe housekeeping. In the future this may change as several hotels in Japan are replacing front desk personnel with robots (Herzfeld, 2018).

You start to realize that because the revenue streams and the cost structure are different, you will want to use different indicators. For MC, serving food and beverage, the cost of sales percentage, was a very important performance metric. But for a hotel cost of sales is not the biggest item: payroll is, so payroll percentage becomes more important. Also, for restaurants, indicators like average food check (AFC), and seat turnover are important vital signs. But for a hotel, average daily rate (ADR) and occupancy are important. Wow, you start to understand business from a financial point of view. You can't wait to begin your professional career.

References

Big Mac purchasing power index by The Economist. Available online at www.statista.com/statistics/274326/big-mac-index-global-prices-for-abig-mac/ (accessed 11 November 2018).

Herzfeld, E. (2018). "Eight more robot-staffed Henn na Hotels to open across Japan". 8 February 2018, available online at www.hotelmanagement.net/tech/eight-more-robot-staffed-henn-na-hotels-to-open-across-japan (accessed 12 November 2018).

Johnson, H. (2018). "We tried the kiosks that analysts say could help McDonald's win back $2.7 billion in sales. Here's the verdict". *Business Insider*, 26 July 2018, available online at www.businessinsider.nl/mcdonalds-kiosk-vs-cashiers-photos-2018-3/?international=true&r=US (accessed 11 November 2018).

Lutz, A. (2015). "How much it costs to eat at every major fast food chain". 4 September 2015, available online at www.businessinsider.com/cost-to-eatat-every-major-fast-food-chain-2015-9?international=true&r=US&IR=T (accessed 22 November 2018).

McDonald's Annual Report 2017. Available from the Electronic Data Gathering, Analysis, and Retrieval system (EDGAR) of the Securities Exchange Commission, available online at www.sec.gov/ix?doc=/Archives/edgar/data/63908/000006390818000010/mcd-12312017x10k.htm (accessed 11 June 2018).

Regus Annual Report 2017. Available online at http://assets.regus.com/investors/annual-reports/2017/2018.04.27-regus-plc-consolidated-report-and-accounts-2017.pdf#_ga=2.54564971.1391206963.1531248233-1598323599.1531248233 (accessed 10 July 2018).

Scandic Hotels Annual Report 2017. Available online at www.scandichotelsgroup.com/annualreports/2017/en/pdf/full.9d186c3.pdf (accessed 12 October 2018).

Singapore Airlines Annual Report 2017. Available online at http://infopub.sgx.com/FileOpen/SIA%20Annual%20Report%202017-18.ashx?App=Announcement&FileID=512720 (accessed 18 August 2018).

Vapiano Annual Report 2017. Available from Deutsche Börse database, available online at http://ir.vapiano.com/download/companies/vapiano/Hauptversammlung/VapianoGB2017_gross_en.pdf (accessed 2 May 2019).

Vapiano Investor Information 2018. Available online at http://ir.vapiano.com/download/companies/vapiano/VeranstaltungenDownloads/201803_Investor_Presentation.pdf (accessed 22 November 2018).

Wilson, P. (2017). *Almanac of Business and Industrial Financial Ratios*. Riverwoods, IL: CCH Publications, Wolters Kluwer.

Notes

1 The case is completely fictional. Any resemblance to a real fries shop or any other establishment, in or outside of Nanaimo, Canada, is purely and entirely coincidental.

2 The Instructor Resources for this book include the raw data for this case.

3 As many McDonald's restaurants are franchised to local businesses, you want to make sure to calculate cost of sales on revenue of McDonald's owned restaurants. Franchised restaurants report their own revenue and cost of sales.

CHAPTER

3 Pricing

Learning outcomes

At the end of this chapter, readers should:

- understand that many disciplines have something to say about pricing, and that pricing decisions in business are ideally the result of a multi-disciplinary effort;
- distinguish between the main accounting cost approaches to pricing and describe their application;
- appreciate how modern-day pricing in the hospitality industry bears little resemblance to the traditional, cost-based accounting approach;
- understand the main financial "cost-volume-profit" considerations involved in organising an event.

THEORY

John Mackillop and Han Yu

Introduction

Pricing is complicated – and emotive. If prices are too expensive, the company may suffer reputational damage and people simply stop buying their product/services. Price too cheaply and you fail to cover costs and go broke. In 1959 the iconic Mini car was launched by the British Motor Company. The Mini was an instant success, and many celebrities of the time owned one. Rival manufacturers each bought a Mini in order to disassemble it and work out how exactly it was made. The competition could not for the life of them work out how BMC were able to manufacture the Mini and sell it for a profit. As it turned out, neither could BMC! The company were so disorganized that they were clueless about how much each car actually cost to manufacture, and were, actually selling each Mini for a loss. And many were sold. Predictably, BMC soon became a hulking, state subsidized shambles, and very quickly disappeared when a free market government took over.

DOI: 10.4324/9781003545903-3

Many fields have a lot to say on the subject of pricing: economics via supply and demand; marketing has a fondness for more psychological techniques, while accounting methods tend to the prosaic, mostly being based on production and overhead costs. However, regardless of method, accounting has to be able to establish that the price is going to be profitable before giving the go ahead.

Economics: supply and demand

Demand is the quantity of a good or service which consumers wish to purchase in a specific time period, e.g. rooms per week, or portions of French fries in a month. As you can appreciate, this quantity varies according to a range of different circumstances: price of the good or service per unit, price of related goods, income levels of the consumers, tastes and fashions, expectations of future prices and so on. *Supply* is the quantity of a good or service which firms are willing to offer for sale, in a certain time period. Again, this quantity supplied varies according to a range of different conditions: price of the good; price of other, related goods; costs of production, levels of technology involved in the supply of the good, and so on.

Generally speaking, consumers wish the price to be as cost effective (cheap) as possible, in order for them to make their incomes go as far as possible, while firms wish the price to be as high as possible, in order to make as much profit as they can. How then can these two apparently opposing priorities be reconciled? Supply and demand provide the solution to this conundrum.

In Figure 3.1, point E is the equilibrium, in other words it represents the price at which the amount which consumers wish to buy is the same as the

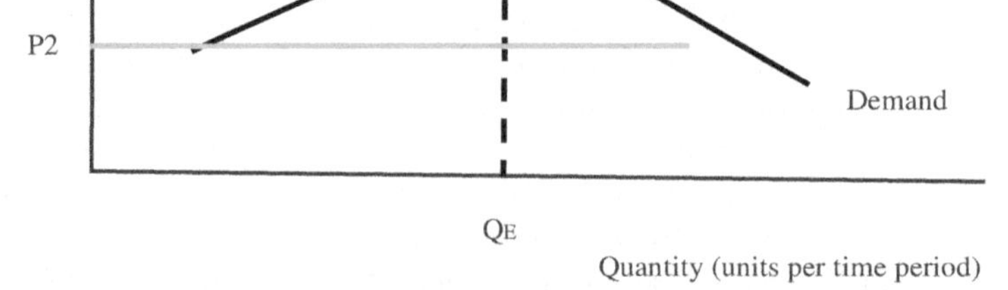

Figure 3.1 Supply and demand equilibrium

amount which firms wish to supply. The eagle eyed among you will realise that the equilibrium is a unique point, and that any price above or below E, will result in either a shortage or surplus of supply relative to demand.

For example, at P1, consumers consider the price to be rather expensive, and either forgo consumption altogether, or opt for some alternative. This P1 is a hotel with an occupancy rate of, say, 26%, or a desolate, near empty restaurant on a weekend evening. This surplus of supply over demand would cause firms to gradually reduce prices – which causes incremental increases in demand – until eventually equilibrium is once more restored at E, the point where supply and demand are in balance. At P2, on the other hand, consumers consider they have a bargain, and purchase large quantities of the good/service. A hotel charging such a low rate might experience that not only the current, but also the next high season would already be fully booked. Firms are not particularly interested in supplying this item, given that a lower price, all other things being equal, will reduce profits. Firms therefore move resources to the supply of other items whose price has not fallen. This causes a shortage, and consumers bid up prices, causing firms to gradually increase supply until equilibrium is restored once more.

Supply and demand determine the average room rates in a particular area. In the aftermath of the September 11 attacks of 2001, room ADR nose-dived as demand plunged. However, in subsequent years it was occupancy that took the hit, as marketers persuaded hoteliers to maintain prices in order to protect brand equity. This left many properties up at price P1 in Figure 3.1.

Price elasticity of demand (PED)

In economics, PED is essentially a measure of how responsive demand is to a change in price. In some instances, elasticity is low, and price rises or falls elicit a relatively small change in demand. In other areas, a price change brings about a relatively large change in demand.

In Figure 3.2, an identical price rise in each market brings about a significantly different response in terms of rooms sold per month. In market A the fall in demand is small, even negligible, while in B the drop in business is potentially ruinous. Market A is classified as Inelastic Demand, while B is Elastic Demand.

$$\text{Equation:} \frac{\text{Percentage change in quantity demanded}}{\text{Percentage change in price}}$$

The reason that business is so interested in PED, is that in a market characterized by inelastic demand, to raise the price is to increase revenue, and to lower the price is to lower revenue, while in a market with elastic demand, the opposite is true. This is why large organisations calculate PED to within

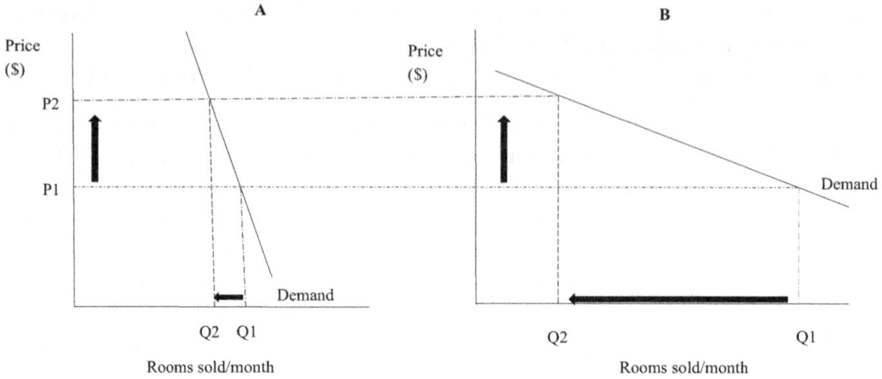

Figure 3.2 Price elasticity of demand

two decimal points (e.g. 1.56, or 0.38) in order to try and predict the revenue impact of a price change.

There are a number of determinants of PED, such as the price as a percentage of income (shoes versus house prices); however, the most significant factor is the number and availability of close substitutes. Companies with little competition, e.g. in remote areas, are able to take advantage of inelastic demand by cranking prices up, while properties in crowded holiday resorts, are having to compete like rats in a sack keeping prices competitively low. This is one of the reasons hotels are so eager to try and differentiate themselves from the competition, in an effort to distance themselves from their main competitors and thus reduce their PED.

Price discrimination

Somewhat surprisingly, the rooms division of a hotel sets prices according to demand, has high fixed costs, low variable costs, and changes prices fairly frequently; whereas F&B pricing is normally based on costs (with high variable costs) and prices tend to be quite stable. In fact, many people staying in the same hotel, in the same type of room, on the same night, will probably be paying a different price. This is known as yield or revenue management. The topic is discussed (Josephi and Melissen, 2017) in Chapter 10 of *Hotel Accommodation Management*, another volume in this Hospitality Essentials Series. The concept has its roots in economics, is known as price discrimination, and will be outlined briefly here. Price discrimination is when a firm charges different prices for the same service, either to different customer segments (business travellers, students etc.), or to the same customers at different times. It is based on the idea that different customers have a different willingness (and ability) to pay.

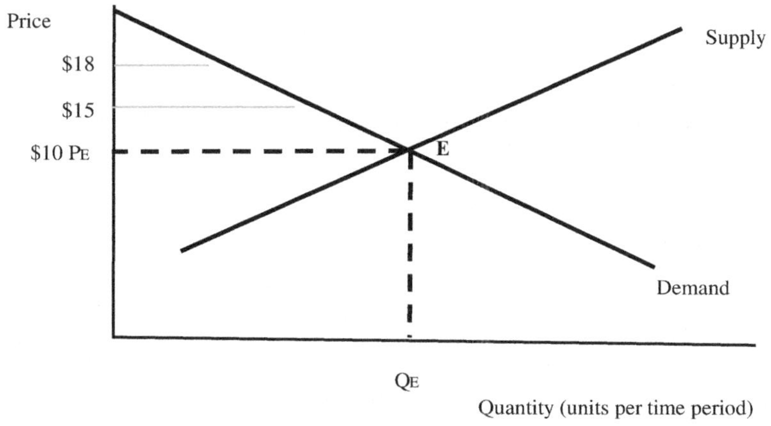

Figure 3.3 Price discrimination

Returning to Figure 3.2, it is clear that demand in A is more inelastic (or less elastic, if you prefer), meaning they would be charged a higher price for exactly the same service, e.g. a hotel room or a plane seat. The business traveller has to get to their meeting, and the company is picking up the tab anyway. Demand in B is much more elastic, say leisure travel, and plans can be altered or shelved in the face of high prices. If members of B were able to sell on their tickets to those in A, the whole thing simply wouldn't work.

The whole point of price discrimination is that it allows firms to reduce Consumer Surplus, an area of the Supply and Demand diagram they have long viewed with an avaricious eye; see Figure 3.3. Here the market equilibrium price is $10, which is what everybody is asked to pay. However, there are some who are willing and able to pay $15, others $18 and so on and so forth. However they are only being charged $10. This consumer surplus is the bonus received by those who would have gladly paid more. Price discrimination is all about being able to identify, separate and charge customers based on their willingness and ability to pay.

Issues with the economic approach

Clearly, the economic approach has its limitations. Not many companies have the technical wherewithal to be able to calculate their supply and demand curves with any great degree of accuracy. And even if they did manage to make a reasonable fist of it, would it really be able to provide them with an accurate equilibrium price? Even then we don't have enough information. How profitable is this equilibrium price? What are the underlying unit costs, which are vital in order to establish unit profitability? Unfortunately, economics is uncharacteristically quiet on the subject.

Marketing: psychological pricing

Mainstream economic theory would have us believe that we humans behave in a rational way, only engaging in an activity/purchase if the marginal (extra) *benefit* – both financial and psychological – as a result of so doing exceeds the marginal *cost* of so doing. We do not consciously go about our business muttering about marginal costs and marginal benefits, yet we conduct ourselves in this sensible, rational, analytical way. On the other hand, Behavioural Economics, effectively a hybrid of economics and psychology, says: "Hang on a minute, we're not actually that smart, and can quite easily be fooled into behaving in ways in which the skilled marketer wants us to". It would go too far to mention all marketing and psychological pricing techniques here, but let us consider one example of each.

"Skim the Cream Pricing" refers to the sometimes very high prices charged by companies when a new product or service is launched. In many cases, there will be people out there who are prepared to pay these very high prices and ensure that so many new products are able to survive to the growth and maturity phase, where the rest of us tend to buy them. In marketing parlance, they are referred to as innovators and early adopters. Think of those lines of Apple fans lined up in their sleeping bags waiting for the doors to open and surge in to snap up the latest iPhone.

There is a wonderful example of the power of Psychological pricing in *Principles of Marketing* (Kotler and Armstrong, 2010). Some years ago, Smirnoff held the largest market share in the US vodka market. Then along came Wolfschmidt Vodka: they claimed that not only would they take "the Pepsi Challenge" against Smirnoff any day of the week, but that Wolfschmidt were also cheaper. The clear implication was that Smirnoff had been taking advantage of their brand leading position, to charge a very high price. Smirnoff couldn't very well reduce their prices as this would be tantamount to admitting Wolfschmidt were right. What they did was pure genius. They *raised* the price of their main brand by $1, introduced a Premium brand for another dollar more, and launched a cheap and cheerful rotgut version, for, you've guessed it, even less than Wolfschmidt. What this did at a stroke, was to reposition Wolfschmidt in the eyes of vodka drinkers, as a cheap brand drunk by those who liked to drink but didn't have much money.

Often, companies combine ("bundle") a number of products and sell them as a job lot at a significantly lower price than you would pay for buying each item individually. For example, a stay at a spa hotel could include room, dinner, spa treatments, and a (half) bottle of Champagne. The point is to increase profits despite the discount being offered per item. It is found regularly in many industries, e.g. mobile phone deals bundling together, calls, texts and data, fast food restaurants offering burger, fries and a soft drink, and on-line travel agents offering all-inclusive holiday packages.

Another issue companies may encounter when establishing prices is the information asymmetry between them and their customers, which could make for an adverse selection problem. This problem was famously discussed by Akerlof (1970) in his article "The market for 'lemons'", using a hypothetical used car market as an example. Imagine the current conditions of the cars for sale in such a market would vary considerably: some are "peaches", others "lemons". There are currently ten used cars for sale. Five of them – the peaches – are in good condition and worth $20,000 each. The other five – the lemons – are in bad condition and only worth $5,000 each. The problem: potential buyers walking into this market would not be able to tell the peaches from the lemons. Only the sellers of the cars know the conditions of each car. If all the buyers are rational decision makers who seek to maximize their own benefits, they would pay no more than $12,500 to get a car in this market, which is the average value of all the cars in the market. Otherwise, they risk losing money. But for a mere $12,500 the sellers of the peaches will not sell their cars. Only the sellers of the lemons would be interested in selling at that price point. The rational buyers with the budget to protect themselves from losing money will only get bad cars instead of good ones, which is called adverse selection.

To prevent the problem of adverse selection, sellers can send a "signal" to their potential buyers to show the quality of their products. In our used car market, sellers can get the cars examined by a third party and obtain a certificate for the conditions of their cars. With such a certificate, the sellers of the good cars can ask a higher price for their cars. This practice of signaling (Spence, 1973) can reduce information asymmetry between two parties. You are studying in a university to get a diploma to show potential employers your professional competencies, so that you can "price yourself up" by asking a higher salary. Hospitality businesses do the same. They get themselves certified with "stars" or "diamonds" by rating organizations to show potential customers their service quality. Or they carefully build up a brand reputation, so that guests know what to expect, and the business can charge the kind of rates they believe match the product's value.

It is important to realize that by setting certain price levels, companies are essentially positioning themselves in the market and targeting certain groups of people. This is particularly important for luxury brands, for which high prices are part and parcel of their brand identity. In this segment, pricing does not rely on manufacturing cost, but on the perceived value of the brand. As a result, luxury brands need to be careful with promotions and reducing prices. People choose luxury lodging and dining not only for the high quality of service and luxury experience, but also for its high-class social recognition. Reducing prices may thus have the unintended effect of lowering the perceived customer value and shifting the customer base from the luxury segment to a more budget-sensitive mid-market segment. In other words, a significant price reduction may very well fail to deliver increased sales, but rather position the product differently.

Issues with the marketing/psychological approach

These are twofold, and relate in general terms to costs and integrity. As with economic techniques, marketing/psychological pricing ignores any real consideration of costs. Prices are charged according to how much the customer can be persuaded to part with, rather than establishing unit costs and then applying a profit margin, with the result that there is no coherent idea regarding how profitable each individual sale actually is. The second issue is that many businesses these days claim to be "sustainable", i.e. they are responsible and caring members of society, and have an honest, and mutually beneficial relationship with their customer base. The problem with our marketing/psychological methods is that they tend to rely on taking advantage of our not being as smart as we like to think we are. How can firms possibly reconcile these two opposing philosophies?

Accounting techniques

Now at last, we come to pricing methods which take costs into account. Accounting has long held the moral high-ground where pricing is concerned, focusing on calculating the cost of providing each unit, whether it be a meal, room, or drink, and adding a mark-up which represents a "fair profit". This is in direct contrast to the techniques outlined in the previous section.

Generally speaking, costs can be divided into two main categories, fixed and variable. Fixed costs (sometimes known as overhead costs) stay the same regardless of level of output, or number of guests served, e.g. interest payments, rent, property taxes and insurance, and administration costs. Variable costs, on the other hand, do vary with output and include wages (not salaries), food, drinks, cleaning materials, part-time staff and so on. Chapter 4, "Finance and accounting in F&B", has some more detail about how costs behave as a function of sales. In this section we shall look at *full-cost pricing*, where all relevant costs are taken into account; *variable-cost pricing*, which is just what it says on the tin, in that only variable costs are taken into account; and *return on investment pricing* where we look at pricing through the eyes of the "Hubbart Formula". As in previous sections, we shall attempt to point out the limitations of and problems with each method.

Full-cost pricing

Here, firms simply sum up all the fixed and variable costs together and then add on an agreed mark up, or profit margin, giving you the selling price. Many firms have a standard, or "house" profit margin, used in each division

Table 3.1 Standard mark-up pricing

Fixed costs per unit of output	\$40
Variable costs per unit	\$100
Total cost per unit	\$140
Profit margin at 20% of total costs	\$28
Price	\$168

or department, a fixed percentage which they add on to the entire product or service line in area of operation. This is a very popular pricing method, maybe the most frequently used in the world, mainly due to it being simple to understand. A simple example illustrates how it works. A firm applies a mark-up of 20% to total costs in order to calculate prices.

Now, at last, firms and customers have a simple, straightforward, and honest pricing method (in contrast to some of the marketing approaches discussed in the previous section). Unfortunately, things are not as simple as they seem. For a start, how do we know what our fixed costs per unit are? One of accounting's more confusing statements is that "fixed costs are variable, and variable costs are fixed". Let us explore this by looking at an example. A small family-run 40-room hotel is open all year round. Variable costs per room are \$20 and total overheads \$1.2m. Rooms division absorbs 70% of the overheads and occupancy for the forthcoming year is expected to be 65%. Let's ask ourselves:

- If the hotel applies a full cost mark-up of 20%, how much would they charge per room?
- How much would they charge if occupancy was expected to be 55%?

At 65% occupancy, total rooms sold = 40 rooms × 365 days × 0.65 occupancy = 9,490 rooms sold per year.
Overhead per room = (0.7 × 1.2 million) / 9,490 = \$88.52
Total Cost per room = \$88.52 overhead + \$20 variable cost = \$108.52
Price charged for a room = \$108.52 × 1.2 (20% mark-up) = (rounded) \$130 per room

This is relatively straightforward and we can see the cost and profit figures quite clearly. Profit per room is \$130 minus total cost per room of \$108.52, giving us a figure of \$21.48. However, things get a bit more complicated when we take a look at the second question.

At 55% occupancy, total rooms = 40 rooms × 365 days × 0.55% occupancy = 8,030 rooms
Overhead per room = (0.7 × 1.2 million) / 8,030 = \$104.61
Total Costs = \$104.61 + \$20 = \$124.61
Price charged for a room = \$124.61 × 1.2 = (rounded) \$150 per room

Now this is a bit confusing. By applying total cost mark-up techniques, we see that the hotel is now asking a higher price, up from $130, with an expected 65% occupancy, to $150 with 55% occupancy. This flies in the face of accepted economic wisdom, where low demand is equated with a low price, and higher demand with a higher price. The problem here is that, when confronted by a fall in demand, the response of a firm blindly practicing full-cost pricing would be to raise prices.

This is shown in Figure 3.4: occupancy in Question 1 is represented by demand curve D1, with an equilibrium Price of P1 and Q1 rooms sold. However, at the start of Question 2, demand has fallen to D2, so the new equilibrium price should be P2, with Q2 the new lower occupancy. If the firm follows the process of pricing based on calculating unit costs as outlined in the answer to Question 2, they will raise the price to P3, resulting in a surplus of rooms to the tune of B minus A. This is a very poor level of occupancy which requires drastic action – and certainly not a price hike. So it looks as if the full-cost method is not as fool-proof and clear cut as we thought.

This higher price is caused by there now being fewer rooms over which to spread the overhead. These fixed costs – e.g. the mortgage, property taxes, depreciation – are not going to fall as demand drops. So the overhead of $840,000 which was spread over 9,490 rooms at 65% occupancy, is now having to be paid by a mere 8,030 rooms. In order to get round this problem, firms frequently try and establish a "normal level of output" on which to base

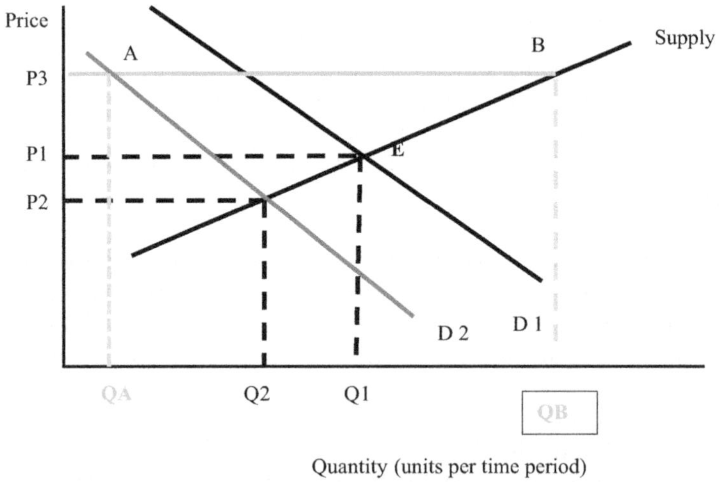

Figure 3.4 Supply and demand equilibrium using full-cost method

their cost and price calculations. However, this is not particularly feasible in the hospitality industry where demand varies on a daily, weekly, monthly, seasonal and annual basis, and indeed in the restaurant business on an hourly basis. Unfortunately, there is yet another, equally problematic issue with full-cost pricing. For this we need to visit the thorny issue of Overhead Allocation, sometimes known as Absorption Costing.

Allocation of overheads

From a full-cost pricing perspective the problem is that fixed costs are frequently indirect in nature, meaning they can be quite hard to trace to the point where they are actually incurred. For example, how much of the total HR bill, or administration costs, or HQ costs, should be paid for out of the rooms' division pot? This is very hard to calculate – notwithstanding that there is an entire area of costing, Activity Based Costing, devoted to the topic. You will be relieved to read that ABC is beyond the remit of this modest tome.

Let's explore the problem using the following example. A local company runs the restaurant and gift shop in a small hospital. Financial information for the last month, a fairly typical one, is laid out in Table 3.2.

Note that the term contribution refers to how much each department's revenue contributes, or pays towards, fixed costs and ultimately profits, once all variable costs have been paid. Contribution shall be discussed more fully in the Variable Cost Pricing section.

In order to provide a clear idea of how much each department is contributing to Operating Profit, the company needs to be able to allocate overhead costs to both the restaurant and the gift shop. There are a number of ways of doing this. Let us begin by allocating costs according to the percentage sales of each department. If we do this, we get the following. Restaurant sales are 277,500 divided by 370,000 = 75% of total sales, which means the gift shop's sales comprise 25% of the total. This means that the restaurant

Table 3.2 Financial information, restaurant and gift shop

	Restaurant ($)	*Gift shop ($)*	*Total ($)*
Sales	277,500	92,500	370,000
– Variable Costs	182,000	76,000	258,000
= Contribution	95,500	16,500	112,000
– Overhead			72,000
= Operating profit			40,000

must pay \$72,000 × 0.75 = \$54,000 of the overhead, while the gift shop must pay \$72,000 × 0.25 = \$18,000. We can illustrate this in Table 3.3.

Table 3.3 Using percentage of sales to allocate overhead expenses

	Restaurant (\$)	*Gift shop (\$)*	*Total (\$)*
Sales	277,500	92,500	370,000
– Variable Costs	182,000	76,000	258,000
= Contribution	95,500	16,500	112,000
– Overhead	54,000	18,000	72,000
= Operating profit	41,500	(1,500)	40,000

This suggests that the gift shop is in fact a drag on the business, and that, if this is representative of a fairly typical month, then perhaps the firm should consider either closing it down or divesting themselves of it. Or does it? Let us try another way of allocation overheads. This time we use the amount of equipment in each premises as a method of allocating the overhead. Assume the restaurant has \$255,000 worth of equipment, while the gift shop has \$45,000, making for a total of \$300,000.

This gives us: restaurant's share of the overhead = 255,000 / 300,000 = 85%. We now multiply the total overhead of \$72,000 by 0.85 to get \$61,200 which is the share now paid by the restaurant. The gift shop now pays 45,000 / 300,000 = 15%, which amounts to \$10,800.

Table 3.4 Using the amount of equipment to allocate overhead expenses

	Restaurant (\$)	*Gift shop (\$)*	*Total (\$)*
Sales	277,500	92,500	370,000
– Variable costs	182,000	76,000	258,000
= Contribution	95,500	16,500	112,000
– Overhead	61,200	10,800	72,000
= Operating profit	34,300	5,700	40,000

We see in Table 3.4 that, simply by changing the method of allocating the overhead, the gift shop is now making a nice little monthly profit. Note that all we have done is use another, equally valid way of allocating the exact same overhead to each department. We could also use criteria such as floor space or number of employees in both departments, and they would all, provided the relative percentage figures are different, give us a different amount of overheads payable by each department, and a different operating profit. In actual fact, in larger companies different overheads are allocated in different ways, e.g. marketing costs according to percentage sales, administration costs according to number of employees or payroll, and maintenance according to floor space or value of equipment. As you can see there is an element of guesswork/rule of thumb here, especially as some marketing, administration and maintenance costs are not readily associated with a specific area of activity.

Additionally, firms tend to experience lower average costs per unit of output (per guest) as the company grows in size and output rises. Grateful suppliers provide substantial discounts, banks provide loans more readily and at a lower rate of interest, and the return per marketing dollar spent is higher. This is known as economies of scale. The result is that as costs per unit fall, then so should the full-cost mark up, provided it is being applied assiduously, and result in ever falling prices. Clearly this is at odds with a firm's desire to continually increase profits, which implies that an element of discretion is applied to the full-cost pricing model.

Variable cost pricing

Otherwise known as the Contribution Method, or Marginal Cost Pricing, this method simply involves calculating the variable cost per unit and applying a mark up to arrive at a price. An obvious advantage is the relative simplicity of calculating variable costs as opposed to full costs. However, while no one disputes that in the long term, pricing policy must cover full costs in order to ensure corporate profitability, in the short run, this may enable the firm to sell off unsold rooms, or attract new market segments, by offering very low prices. We are straying once more into the area of price discrimination and revenue management, and successful application of variable cost pricing is contingent on the assumption that the main customer base has already paid off the full costs.

We start with a look at the contribution, which was introduced in the full-cost section but not fully explained. We shall do so here, and start by revisiting our restaurant/gift shop example. Remember that the contribution refers to how much is left over after paying all variable costs. This money then goes on to help pay for fixed costs and ultimately profits. Note that in our first example when we allocated overheads according to percentage sales, the restaurant made an operating profit of $41,500 while the gift shop made an operating loss of $1,500 – see Table 3.3. Let us assume that management are not too sophisticated, and decide the gift shop is a liability they could well do without. They decide to cut their losses and *rent out* the gift shop to a third party for the sum of $2,000 per month. They calculate that this will pay off the gift shop's operating losses of $1,500 and give them an extra $500 profit per month, taking total operating profits up to $40,500 per month. However, Table 3.5 below shows what actually happens:

Table 3.5 Gift shop is rented out for $2,000 per month

	Restaurant ($)	*Gift shop ($)*	*Total ($)*
Sales	277,500	2,000	279,500
– Variable costs	182,000		182,000
= Contribution	95,500	2,000	97,500
– Overhead	72,000		72,000
= Operating profit	23,500	2,000	25,500

To management's dismay, total operating profits have, far from rising by $500 per month, actually fallen by a whopping $14,500 per month. How did this happen? The answer is that they didn't realise that the poor little gift shop was actually quietly making a contribution to fixed costs equal to $16,500 per month, and that any rental agreement must ensure that this contribution was covered, otherwise profits would fall. This is an important point, and many small firms mistakenly divest themselves of apparently unprofitable departments by failing to take the contribution INTO account. Remember, also, that the only reason the gift shop was making a loss in the first place, was down to the way in which the overhead was allocated. When equipment value was used, they actually showed a profit.

The concept of contribution is an important one, and allows companies to embark on some highly profitable projects which would not be deemed feasible using full-cost pricing. Remember, however, that overall, a company will not make a profit until all fixed costs have been paid. We will conclude this section with an example showing how to calculate profits using variable cost pricing.

A firm produces and sells 100,000 units of output one year at the following costs:

Direct materials	$250,000
Direct labour	$400,000
General and administration	$310,000
Interest and property taxes	$180,000
Other variable costs	$150,000
Other overhead costs	$110,000

If the firm prices using a mark-up of 80% on variable costs, how much operating profit did they make? At this point it is important not to panic: take a deep breath and simply split the costs between variable and fixed. First the variable:

Direct materials	$250,000
Direct labour	$400,000
Other variable costs	$150,000
Total variable cost:	$800,000

Now that we know our total variable costs we can add the mark-up in order to give us our revenue. We simply multiply the total variable cost by 1.8: $800,000 × 1.8 = $1,440,000.

Now the fixed:

General and administration	$310,000
Interest and property taxes	$180,000
Other overhead costs	$110,000
Total overhead costs	$600,000

Now let's put it all together:

Table 3.6 Variable cost pricing

Sales (100,000 × $14.40)	$1,440,000
– Variable costs	($800,000)
– Overheads	($600,000)
Operating profits	$40,000

All that fuss for an operating profit of $40,000. However, the point is that, as variable costs per unit are relatively stable compared with fixed costs per unit, using variable costs gives us a more solid base on which to add the mark-up. Generally speaking, variable costs give a company the lowest limit at which a price can be set in the short run, and still contribute towards profits – often quite substantially so. However, in the long run, firms must be able to cover all costs, both fixed and variable, while providing a margin of profit acceptable to management and shareholders.

Desired ingredient cost mark-up (DICMU)

This is an extreme form of variable cost pricing and is very popular in the restaurant industry. Very simple, it involves restaurants having a mark-up which they apply to the ingredient costs of a given plate of food, e.g. by applying a multiple of 4 to the ingredient costs to arrive at the menu price. This method is very easy to calculate, which to some extent accounts for its popularity.

Return on investment pricing: the Hubbart formula

This, our final pricing method involves turning the P&L on its head. It starts with a desired level of net profit, and works its way back to calculate what the required Rooms revenues must be in order to generate this figure. In fact, it goes back even further, and asks "What is the required Average Daily Rate (ADR), given an expected occupancy level, that will give us this profit?"

A simplified example should help make things clear. The owners of a 400-room hotel desire an annual return on investment of 20% on an initial investment of $5,000,000. What is the required Average Daily Rate?

- Tax on profits is 20%
- The hotel has $10 million of debt, on which they pay 15% interest
- Depreciation and undistributed operating expenses are estimated to be $4,250,000
- Other operated departments' income: $500,000
- Rooms department direct expenses $4,000,000
- Occupancy level for the forthcoming year is assumed to be 65%

Desired net profit 20% of $5,000,000	$1,000,000
Requires a pre-tax profit of 1,000,000 / (1 –0.20) =	$1,250,000
Add interest payments = $10,000,000 × 0.15 =	$1,500,000
Which gives us required *EBIT*	$2,750,000
Add depreciation + undistributed operating expenses	$4,250,000
Which gives us required *departmental income*	$7,000,000
Subtract other departments' income	$500,000
Which gives us required *Rooms income*	$6,500,000
Add Rooms department direct expenses	$4,000,000
Which gives us required *Rooms revenue*	$10,500,000
Estimated number of rooms sold = 400 × 365 × 0.65 =	94,900
Average room rate = $10,500,000 / 94,900 =	$110.64

All of this tells us that, provided our cost and occupancy forecasts are accurate, in order to generate an annual return on investment equal to 20%, our firm must sell $10.5m worth of rooms at an average rate of $110.64. Let's go crazy and say $111. Hand this over to your Revenue Management and Sales colleagues and let them get on with it!

Conclusion

In this theory section, we have seen how the fields of economics, marketing, with their focus on psychology, and accounting address the crucial topic of pricing. As stated in the introduction, get pricing wrong and you are in trouble: price too high and customers will eventually notice and become alienated; while on the other hand pricing too low for too long, will end you in bankruptcy court.

Bibliography

Akerlof, G. A. (1970). "The Market for 'Lemons': Quality Uncertainty and the Market Message in Words: Because I DO like it! Mechanism". *Quarterly Journal of Economics*, 84(3), 488–500. https://doi.org/10.2307/1879431.

Glautier, M. W. E. and Underdown, B. (2011). *Accounting Theory and Practice.* Harlow: Pearson Education.

Gowthorpe, C. (2011). *Business Accounting and Finance.* Hampshire: Cengage Learning.

Josephi, S. and Melissen, F. (2017). Hotel Revenue Management. In R. C. Wood (ed.) *Hotel Accommodation Management*, Abingdon: Routledge.

Kotler, P. and Armstrong, G. (2010). *Principles of Marketing*, 13th, Global edition. New Jersey: Pearson.

Mankiw, N. G., Taylor, M. P. and Ashwin, A. (2016). *Business Economics*, 2nd edition. Hampshire: Cengage Learning.

Nolen-Hoeksema S., Fredrickson L. B., Loftus G. L. and Lutz C. (2015). *Atkinson & Hilgard's Introduction to Psychology*, 16th edition. Boston: Cengage Learning.

Schmidgall, R. S. (2017). *Hospitality Industry Managerial Accounting.* Lansing: AHLEI.

Sloman, J. and Jones, E. (2017). *Essential Economics for Business*, 5th edition. Harlow: Pearson.

Spence, Michael. (1973). "Job Market Signaling2. *The Quarterly Journal of Economics*, 87(3), 355–374.

PRACTICE: THE SEOUL ULTIMATE DANCE SHINDIG

Jur van de Graaf

Introduction

A team of event organizers is working together to organize the first edition of the "Seoul Ultimate Dance Shindig".[1] They are driven by a profound passion for culture, and an unwavering love for dance. Brimming with ideas to enhance the cultural vibrancy of the Korean capital, they have crafted a sound master plan for the event. As part of that plan, they have translated all of their ideas into a detailed budget. This case will explore the team's financial considerations in terms of pricing and costing out this event.

Cost structure of the event

The Seoul Ultimate Dance Shindig (SUDS) is a not-for-profit organization. However, as the organizers plan to organize the event for a number of years, they cannot afford to take too much financial risk which might result in substantial losses.

A major part of the event budget is the fixed costs – that is, costs that are not a function of the number of visitors. An example of fixed costs is the DJs: the fees are agreed upon for playing the set, regardless of how many visitors actually show up. Virtually all costs for an event such as SUDS are fixed. Not only the DJs, but also the rent of the venue, the marketing for the event, all other organization expenses: they all need to be planned and paid for regardless of how many people will eventually show up! Usually, the major exception is the cost of sales. More visitors lead to more sales of food and beverages (F&B), which means higher costs of sales.

SUDS have created the following budget, based on 4,500 visitors attending the event (all amounts in Korean Won):

Table 3.7 Seoul Ultimate Dance Shindig 1st Edition budget

	₩
Revenue from ticket sales	270,000,000
Revenue from F&B sales	135,000,000
Total revenue	**405,000,000**
Cost of sales F&B	49,500,000
Total cost of sales	**74,500,000**
Gross profit	**355,500,000**
Programming costs	150,000,000
Production costs	80,000,000
Ticket sales transaction costs	25,000,000
Other variable operating costs	31,500,000
Other fixed operating costs	40,000,000
Total operating costs	**326,500,000**
Operating profit	**29,000,000**
Event insurance	5,000,000
Profit for the event	**24,000,000**

The organizers have determined that *Cost of sales F&B* and *Other variable operating costs* are variable. All other costs are fixed, resulting in the following cost structure:

- Total revenue ₩405,000,000
- Total fixed costs ₩300,000,000
- Total variable costs ₩81,000,000

The organizers are satisfied that they have managed to draft a budget with an expected profit. However, they are aware that there is a possibility that fewer than 4,500 visitors will attend this first SUDS edition. Therefore, they need to know the minimum number of visitors required to prevent them from making a loss. That minimum number of visitors is the *break-even point*. The break-even point is the moment where income equals costs, resulting in neither profit nor loss.

Calculating the break-even point

Now that the budget has been drafted, the break-even point can be calculated. The organizers start with asking themselves the question: what if there are no visitors at all? In that case, all fixed costs would still be incurred, whereas both revenue and variable cost are ₩0. In other words, this would result in a net loss of ₩300,000,000.

Every ₩1 realized in revenue contributes to covering these fixed costs. When all fixed costs are covered, the event breaks even. However, an increase in revenue also leads to an increase in variable costs. In their calculations, they first need to deduct variable costs from revenue before they can start covering the fixed costs. The amount of variable costs relative to revenue is called the *contribution margin*.

Looking at their budget, revenue – variable costs = ₩405,000,000 – ₩81,000,000 = ₩324,000,000. As a relative proportion of revenue, that is ₩324,000,000/₩405,000,000 = 80%. So, 80% of revenue can be used to cover the fixed costs. Or to make this more concrete: with every ₩100 realized in revenue, an additional ₩20 in variable costs is incurred, so ₩80 remain to cover the fixed costs.

$$Contribution\ margin\left(\%\right)=\frac{\left(Revenue-Variable\,Costs\right)}{Revenue}$$

Now that they know the contribution margin, they can relate this figure to total fixed costs. The break-even point is calculated by dividing the fixed costs by the contribution margin. ₩300,000,000 / 0.80 = ₩375,030,000. This is the revenue required to break even.

$$\text{Breakeven point} = \frac{\text{Fixed Costs}}{\text{Contribution Margin}}$$

The event organizers find this number quite abstract. They plan with the number of visitors in mind rather than revenue. Since the 4,500 visitors result into revenue of ₩405,000,000, the average revenue per visitor is ₩405,000,000 / 4,500 = ₩90,000. Dividing this amount into the break-even revenue results in ₩375,030,000 / ₩90,000 or 4,167 visitors. In other words, if fewer than 4,167 visitors attend, the event makes a loss. If more than 4,167 visitors show up, the event makes a profit.

Profit markup

Even though making a profit is not the ultimate goal of the organizers, neither is breaking even: any profits SUDS might generate would be more than welcome and would allow the team to make the event even better in the years to come. They agree on a profit of ₩50,000,000 as the financial goal – higher than the currently budgeted profit level of ₩24,000,000.

Any won of revenue above the break-even point comes with additional variable costs. Once the break-even point is reached, profit grows with the pace of the contribution margin. To calculate the additional revenue required, the profit markup is divided by contribution margin: ₩50,000,000 / 0.80 = ₩62,500,000. This amount is added to the break-even revenue, resulting in a required total revenue of ₩437,530,000, or 4,862 visitors.

Setting the sales price

Based on their experience with similar events, the organizers think that 4,500 visitors is more realistic than the 4,862 required to generate ₩50,000,000 of profit. That means that the only way to reach the intended profit level, is to increase revenue per visitor. The revenue of this event is made up of two components: the entry tickets, and the tokens for food and beverages. The tickets are sold for ₩60,000 and the tokens for ₩3,750 each, which means total revenue comprises ticket revenue of ₩270,000,000 and token revenue of ₩135,000,000 (based on 36,000 tokens). The organizers want the event to be accessible to those with lower disposable income, so they do not want to increase the ticket prices. However, they are open to exploring whether the price of the *tokens* could be increased.

The team assumes that as long as they do not raise the token price *too* much, demand for tokens is inelastic, which means that increasing the sales price does not lead to lower sales. The following equation still applies:

$$\text{Revenue} - \text{Variable costs} - \text{Fixed costs} = \text{Profit}$$

The unknown variable in this case is the token sales price. The equation can be rewritten as:

$$(\mathit{Token\ volume} * \mathit{Token\ sales\ price}) + \mathit{Ticket\ revenue} - \mathit{Variable\ costs} - \mathit{Fixed\ costs} = \mathit{Profit}$$

Filling in the known figures:

$$(36{,}000 * \mathit{Token\ sales\ price}) + ₩270{,}000{,}000 - ₩81{,}000{,}000 - ₩300{,}000{,}000 = ₩50{,}000{,}000$$

Rearranging the formula:

$$\mathit{Token\ sales\ price} = \frac{₩161{,}000{,}000}{36{,}000} = ₩4{,}472$$

The sales price of the tokens would have to be increased by almost 20% in order to realize the intended profit level. For now, the organizers find this just a bit too much, and continue to look for alternative options.

Changing the behaviour of costs

Since the event is organized for the first time, it is very uncertain how many visitors will actually show up. Therefore, the organization would like to have a higher proportion of variable costs. That lowers the risk of not reaching the break-even point. After all, if there are no visitors, there are no variable costs. An example would be to pay sales agencies a success fee. Instead of a fixed amount, they are paid a percentage of the ticket sales. The trade-off of this is that if SUDS would prove to be a huge success, the costs would also be higher than budgeted.

The organization can make a deal with the sales agency: instead of paying the fixed amount of ₩25,000,000, the sales agency receives a commission of ₩5,400 per ticket sold. This changes the budgeted amounts to the following:

- Total fixed costs: ₩275,000,000 (instead of ₩300,000,000)
- Variable costs per visitor: ₩23,400 (instead of ₩18,000)
- Revenue per visitor: ₩90,000

Due to this change, the contribution per visitor reduces to ₩66,600. Therefore, the break-even point will change to ₩275,000,000 / ₩66,600 = 4,129 visitors. Compared to the old situation, SUDS now requires 32 visitors less to break even. The trade-off is that profit grows slower as well. To make a profit of ₩50,000,000, the event now requires ₩325,000,000 / ₩66,600 = 4,879 visitors: 18 visitors more than before.

Fixed income

As an additional source of income, the organizers would like to sell merchandising to their visitors. Since they do not have the required expertise and resources in-house, they opt to rent out sales areas at SUDS to third-party vendors. These vendors pay the organizers a fixed amount upfront and retain all sales proceeds. The SUDS team decides to budget ₩20,000,000 as additional income. No additional costs are expected.

The revenue earned from the vendors is independent from the number of visitors, and can be used to cover part of the fixed costs – meaning less fixed costs remain to be covered by the contribution of visitors. Since the revenue from tickets and token sales, and the variable costs all remain the same, this option will lower the break-even point to ₩255,000,000 / ₩66,600 = 3,829 visitors.

Time to dance!

The organizers of SUDS' maiden edition have explored various options to enhance the financial feasibility of the event. They are satisfied with the resulting break-even point of 3,829 visitors, considering this a comfortable margin of safety from the expected 4,500 attendees. As always, uncertainties remain: will visitors spend as much as anticipated? Will all departments stay within budget? Are there any unforeseen costs? Despite these questions, the organizers are confident they have "financially engineered" their event in a responsible way. The lessons learned from this year's event will help refine the budget and calculations for next year's edition.

Note

1 This case is fictional. Any resemblance to existing dance events is purely and entirely coincidental.

CHAPTER

4 Finance and accounting in F&B

Learning outcomes

At the end of this chapter, readers should:

- be able to define key costing concepts and cost behaviours;
- understand the link between strategic plans and an operating budget and appreciate the role both play in planning, controlling and decision-making;
- understand how variance analysis can help deliver operational performance;
- appreciate some of the practical challenges faced by F&B management in this process.

THEORY

James W. Hesford, Craig M. Milner and Michael J. Turner

Introduction

In this chapter we introduce you to accounting concepts that will help you plan and control food and beverage operations. In the next section we define a broad range of cost concepts, introduce four common types of cost behaviour and explain how costs are estimated. Understanding how costs will change as multiple cost drivers change (i.e. number of customers, types of meals ordered, hours of service, etc.) is essential to predicting future spending. And it is these predictions that are necessary to establish an organisational control system that promotes efficiency and minimizes risks associated with employee misappropriation. Budgeting, a quantitative expression of management's expectations for a future course of action, is then discussed. We describe how a sales forecast is created and how these figures are the first step in preparing an operating budget. We then introduce cash budgets that are used to plan for cash collections, cash disbursements and planning for loans. The final topic described is variance analysis, a formal process of quantifying and reporting

DOI: 10.4324/9781003545903-4

how a restaurant's actual results differed from the plan. As most restaurants have low margins, restaurants cannot afford losses due to inefficiency (i.e. wasting resources, employee shirking), employee misappropriation, or a combination of inefficiency and theft. Most businesses fail during a growth phase, suggesting that firms fail to plan or fail to establish effective controls.

Terms and cost behaviour

While preparing financial statements is important for investors, it is arguably more important to provide information to managers who make routine operational decisions and long-term capital investment decisions. For this purpose, the accountant prepares reports relating resource consumption and revenue generation to demand for a firm's products or services. To achieve this goal, accountants use procedures to link one or more drivers of cost with associated spending. In this section, we define accounting terms, classify cost behaviour and describe how to estimate cost functions.

A *cost object* is anything management wants to know the cost of. For example, management may want to know the cost of a product, department, division or customer. Suppose a company wants to evaluate the financial performance of a restaurant. The cost object is the restaurant. The various meals sold are themselves cost objects if management is interested in measuring food cost. To understand cost objects, the accountant must understand how particular products consume resources. A *cost driver* is any factor that causes a cost object's spending, in total, to change.

Costs can be classified in many ways, but the most important is with regard to a cost's behaviour with changes in some cost driver. A *fixed cost* is one that does not change with respect to changes in some cost driver. Assume a restaurant incurs monthly expenses that total $20,000 for rent, depreciation, property taxes, marketing, administration, etc. Since these costs don't change as the restaurant serves more or fewer meals, they are classified as being fixed. This is not to say the cost will not vary – it is possible, and sometimes likely, that a fixed cost will change. But a change *unrelated* to sales volume is still a fixed cost because it is unrelated to the cost driver (meals). For example, a restaurant's rental agreement will have periodic adjustments for property maintenance, insurance and taxes, and the amount of these changes is unknown in advance. The solid line in Figure 4.1 depicts a fixed cost. It is a horizontal line that intercepts the y-axis at $20,000. Conversely, a *variable cost* changes in proportion to a cost driver. One example is the cost of food at a restaurant. Food cost increases as the number of meals increases, and decrease as meals decrease. In the fixed cost example, the cost object is a rental agreement, whereas food cost is the cost object in the example of a variable cost. The dashed line in Figure 4.1 depicts a variable cost. The slope (i.e. steepness, or angle) of the line is known as the unit variable cost. If these were our only two costs and the cost object was the restaurant, the cost object would exhibit a cost behaviour

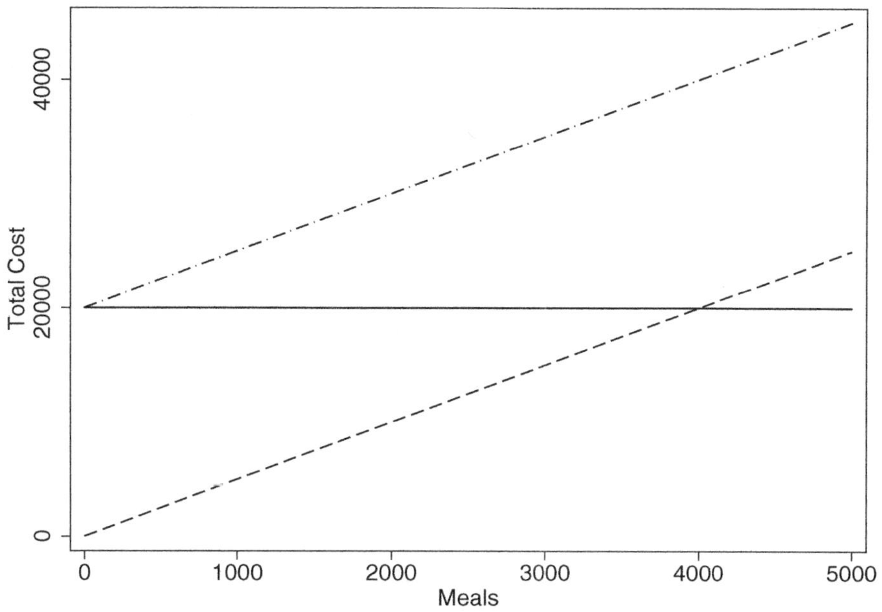

Figure 4.1 Cost behaviour: fixed, variable and total costs

containing both fixed and variable parts. Such cost behaviours are referred to as *mixed costs*. In Figure 4.1, the dash-dot line depicts the mixed cost. These examples (food cost and rent) point out that whether a cost is classified as fixed, variable or mixed often depends on the cost object chosen.

A third type of cost behaviour is a step cost. A *step cost* is a cost that is constant for some range of a cost driver and, at some higher range of the cost driver, the cost increases. Figure 4.2 depicts a step cost. For example, if a restaurant saw its sales volume increase substantially, management may decide to hire an assistant manager. It may also be able to increase seating capacity by expanding into adjacent vacant retail space. In the former example the step cost is reversible (i.e. the assistant manager can be terminated if volume drops), whereas in the latter, the step cost is not reversible (the building owner will not let the restaurant out of a newly-signed rental agreement). These examples make another important point: cost behaviour often depends on the *time horizon*. Over a short period, many costs appear as fixed while over the long run all costs eventually become variable. It is worth mentioning that the cost behaviours described to this point are idealized conceptions.[1]

The mathematical equation that describes cost behaviours is called a *cost equation* or *cost function*. For a fixed cost, total cost (TC) is TC = a. TC = bx is the equation for a variable cost, where b is the variable cost per unit of the cost object and x is a variable representing the number of units of the cost driver

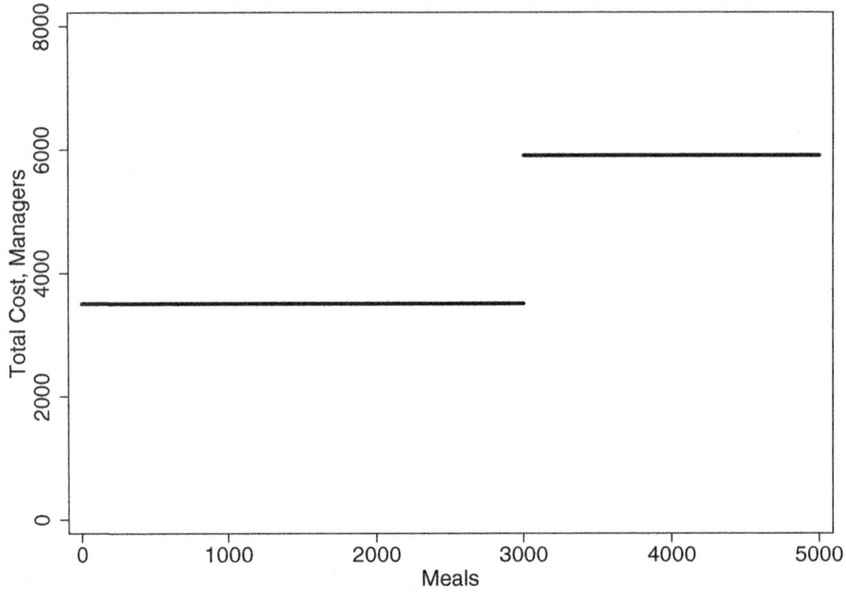

Figure 4.2 Cost behaviour: step cost

(oftentimes this is sales volume, but this depends on the cost object and its cost driver). The equation for a mixed cost, being the sum of fixed and variable costs, is TC = a + bx. These equations are used when preparing budgets, the topic discussed in the next section.

Fixed costs result from decisions made by management and are classified as being either committed or discretionary. *Committed fixed costs* carry some legal obligation for future, periodic payments. Returning to our prior example, a rental contract would constitute a committed fixed cost. Absent a legal obligation, a *discretionary fixed cost* is more easily eliminated. Payments to sponsor a local youth sports team is an example of a discretionary fixed cost. Whether the restaurant seeks publicity or simply wants to contribute to its neighbourhood, it can periodically choose the extent of its support.

Some costs can be associated directly with a particular cost object. This category of costs is referred to as *direct costs*. For example, the cost of beef in a hamburger would be a direct cost as the cost can be *traced* to the cost object. *Indirect costs* are those where we know an association between cost and a cost object exists, but the relationship is unobservable (or not easily observable). For these costs, the management accountant devises a rule to assign the cost to cost objects. The application of these rules is known as *cost allocation*. For example, a restaurant's insurance would be an indirect cost for the hamburger just mentioned. Careful readers will notice that some costs may be indirect for some cost objects, but direct for others. The restaurant's insurance is such an example as this would be a direct cost for the cost object being the entire restaurant. *Cost assignment* is the process of tracing direct costs and allocating indirect costs to cost objects.

Up to this point, the discussion has been about total cost in relation to some cost driver. However, management may want to know the *average cost* of a meal. This average, known as *unit cost*, is simply total cost divided by sales volume. For example, assume total variable cost is $20,000 and monthly fixed cost is $20,000. The restaurant's total cost would be $40,000. If the restaurant served 4,000 meals during the month, the average cost would be $40,000 / 4,000 meals, or $10/meal. If the restaurant served more meals, say 5,000, unit cost would decrease to ($5/meal × 5,000 meals + $20,000) / 5,000 meals = $45,000 / 5,000 meals = $9/meal. Similarly, if fewer meals were served, unit cost would rise. This happens because, while total variable cost changes proportionally with meals, fixed costs are being spread across fewer meals, causing the average to rise. These calculations reveal that unit cost *depends* upon sales volume. If you studied the "Pricing" chapter before this one, you should already be familiar with this. The morale here is that managers should be very cautious when using unit costs. It is almost always best to think in terms of total cost.

Having described total cost and unit cost, we now define *incremental cost*. Incremental cost is the change in cost for the next unit of a cost driver. Imagine, for example, that a delicatessen sells a steak sandwich. The incremental cost includes the cost of the steak, bread and all toppings used in the sandwich. It does not include the cost of labour as the restaurant would not normally pay staff more to make a single sandwich (unless the worker was scheduled to go home and had to stay longer to prepare that next sandwich).[2] Calculating incremental cost simply involves calculating how total spending *changes* when one additional unit of output is produced. Let's imagine that the delicatessen makes fresh bread daily and has a policy of donating excess bread to a homeless shelter at the end of each business day. If a customer comes in and orders a steak sandwich right before closing, and the bread was available (and going to be given to the homeless shelter), the incremental cost would only be the steak and toppings.

Lastly, a short comment on *cost estimation*. In most restaurants, calculating meal cost uses an *industrial engineering*, or work-measurement, method. This method examines the physical association between inputs (e.g. beef, lettuce, tomato, onion, cheese and bun for a cheeseburger) and outputs (i.e. the items produced). For example, assume a steak entrée uses 150 grams of steak at a cost of $80 per kilogram. If the restaurant sells 500 of these entrées, the total cost of the steak would be (500 servings × 150g/serving) / 1,000g/kg × $80/kg = $6,000. The accountant simply repeats these calculations for every output (i.e. menu item) and, when sales forecasts are made, total food cost can be calculated. The process is easy, but tedious.[3]

Strategic plans and budgets

Strategy is a restaurant's goals and the means to achieve them. A strategy stems from a detailed analysis of the current environment (e.g. market trends, customer needs and competitors) and the restaurant's capabilities (e.g. financing, assets, processes and human capital). The resulting *strategic plans* are long-term (three to ten years) visions and forecasts that impact major decisions (e.g. location, size and investment). From these plans, managers create capital budgets (see Chapter 5), operating budgets and cash budgets, the last two of which are described later in this chapter. Budgets are quantitative plans that express a business's future plan of action (i.e. its goals). Operating and cash budgets are usually set for a one-year period, although to further facilitate planning and control, many organisations establish additional budgets at shorter intervals (e.g. quarterly, monthly or weekly). Because sales and costs often vary considerably throughout the year, a short-term budget and regular monitoring of performance is key to long-term success. Many restaurants adopt *rolling budgets*, whereby as one month passes, another month is projected and added to the budget. Rolling budgets ensure a continuous 12-month planning horizon, not limited by annual plans that cover a fiscal year (usually January through December). Without a rolling budget, there would be no planning horizon for the early part of the next year until the next annual plan were to be adopted. The other benefit of a rolling budget is the ability to update the planning horizon as time unfolds.

An important criterion in budget-setting is that short-term goals be in accordance with the long-term strategic plan. Consider a restaurant with a strategic goal of establishing long-term customer satisfaction and retention. While the restaurant may reduce staff and training to boost short-term profit, these actions will likely lead to worse long-term financial performance resulting from decreased customer loyalty and a decline in new customers. To mitigate these issues, budgets are also often used for control purposes (i.e. providing the benchmarks used for assessing what happened during a period of time).

Sales forecast

The first step in preparing a comprehensive operating budget is to create a sales forecast. However, with many variables impacting sales (i.e. season, competition, weather, and special events), forecasting in the food and beverage industry is challenging. Ideally, management draws on historical performance to create a sales forecast, but this is not always possible. For example, a startup restaurant will have to rely on market research, competitive analysis, and recommendations from other professionals (e.g. consultants and accountants).

Forecasting sales is not an exact science, but a common approach is to estimate the number of *covers* (all items purchased by a single person) and the *average check* (spend per cover). The maximum number of covers are primarily determined by a restaurant's capacity (i.e. number of seats in the restaurant) and its ability to quickly reseat a table during busy periods. *Table turns* is a measurement of how many different parties occupy a table over some measurement period. For example, if a restaurant seats 40 and is at capacity for lunch and dinner, with 40 and 60 covers respectively, it will have one table turn for lunch and 1.5 table turns for dinner. Depending on the type of restaurant and market conditions, covers can vary significantly throughout the day and by day of the week. The average check can also exhibit significant variation. Finally, sales don't just originate within the restaurant. Many restaurants will have take-out and/or delivery sales. These sales are also subject to the same variation as in-restaurant sales.

With variability in covers and average check, restaurants typically start with a weekly sales forecast that is "rolled-up" into annual-sales, as well as forecasts by time period, day of week, etc. While established restaurants will use historical data, a start-up restaurant will use market research. Returning to our example, let's assume the restaurant is open daily from 11:00 a.m. to 8:00 p.m. Recall, too, that the restaurant space was designed with capacity for 40 lunch and 60 dinner covers. Assume that management forecasts an average check of $7 for lunch and $12 for dinner. Base weekly sales, as shown in Table 4.1, are calculated as 7 days/week × ($7/lunch cover × 40 lunch covers + $12/dinner cover × 60 dinner covers) = $7,000/week. Take-out and delivery sales are also included, and many restaurants separate weekly sales into "departments" using a percent-of-sales approach. We combine take-out and delivery sales to simplify our examples, but it's common for restaurants to track these as separate departments. Larger restaurants, with multiple seating areas (e.g. restaurant and lounge) might separate sales by seating area. In our example, weekly take-out and delivery was set at 30% ($3,000) of total sales. The weekly sales forecast is used, with a seasonal adjustment, to forecast annual sales by month (see Table 4.2).

Table 4.1 Weekly sales by type

Base weekly sales, restaurant	$7,000	70%
Take-out and delivery	3,000	30%
Total weekly sales	$10,000	100%

Table 4.2 Monthly sales

	Jan.	*Feb.*	*Mar.*	*Apr.*	*May*	*Jun.*	*Jul.*	*Aug.*	*Sep.*	*Oct.*	*Nov.*	*Dec.*
Weeks	4	4	5	4	4	5	4	4	5	4	4	5
Base revenue (000's)	$40	$40	$50	$40	$40	$50	$40	$40	$50	$40	$40	$50
Seasonal adjustment	.80	.80	.80	.90	1.0	1.1	1.1	1.1	1.0	1.0	1.2	1.2
Total (000's)	$32	$32	$40	$36	$40	$55	$44	$44	$50	$40	$48	$60

Note: * The sum of the month totals is a result of "5-week months" being weighted differently.

A monthly sales forecast is useful for financial reporting and performance measurement, but management will likely seek to create additional short-term forecasts. Forecasts by daily time period, daily sales and product mix facilitate short-term operational decision-making and improve understanding of the restaurant.

Most of a restaurant's volume occurs during peak dining periods. In our example, the restaurant is open for lunch and dinner service, but not breakfast. With the restaurant open from 11 a.m. – 8 p.m. there are four time periods usually worth watching: 11 a.m. – 1 p.m. (lunch), 1 p.m. – 5 p.m., 5 p.m. – 6:30 p.m. (dinner) and 6:30 p.m. to close. Once time periods have been established, the percent-of-sales approach can be used to establish a weekly sales target (see Table 4.3).

Sales vary throughout the week and unusual circumstances may result in unusually large (or small) demand on a single day. It's impossible to plan for unusual events, so the intent is to create an expected, or base, sales forecast. Similar to the methodology used for time periods, daily sales are adjusted to account for periods of peak demand and light demand using a percent-of-weekly-sales approach. Continuing with our example, assume that a slow start to the week is anticipated and, because of the restaurant's location to local shopping and entertainment, very strong demand is anticipated on Fridays and Saturdays. Weekly sales by day would look something like Table 4.4.

Many restaurants find it useful to forecast sales by sales mix. Sales mix is the proportion of sales of each item, relative to all items offered by a restaurant.

Table 4.3 Weekly sales, by time period

Period	*Percentage (%)*	*Amount ($)*
Lunch (11 a.m. – 1 p.m.)	45	4,500
Afternoon (1 p.m. – 5 p.m.)	15	1,500
Dinner (5 p.m. – 6:30 p.m.)	30	3,000
Close (6:30 p.m. – 8 p.m.)	10	1,000
Total	100	10,000

Table 4.4 Daily sales

	Mon.	*Tue.*	*Wed.*	*Thu.*	*Fri.*	*Sat.*	*Sun.*
Weekly sales	10%	10%	10%	15%	20%	25%	10%
Daily sales	$1,000	$1,000	$1,000	$1,500	$2,000	$2,500	$1,000

Table 4.5 Weekly sales mix

Mains	55%	$5,500
Sides and salads	20%	$2,000
Beverages	15%	$1,500
Liquor	10%	$1,000
Total	100%	$11,000

Many restaurants will have dozens of items, and the product mix is often calculated for a small number of categories, such as food, beverages, liquor, etc. A large restaurant might have managers for each of these categories and would likely provide forecasts for sub-categories for additional control. Table 4.5 is an example of sales separated into mains, sides and salads, beverages and liquor.

With a detailed sales forecast in place, a restaurant is not only able to build a more accurate operating budget, but better able to understand and manage operational performance.

Operating budget

With the sales forecast completed, it is possible to prepare an *operating budget*. An operating budget is the detailed plan for sales and associated costs. As mentioned previously, the purpose of a budget is to help management understand and control an organisation.

Food cost and labour are a restaurant's largest expense categories. Together, they range from 45–65% of total cost. Given their magnitude, and the low profit margins typical of restaurants, controlling these two expense categories will be critical to ensuring profitability. For this reason, restaurant operating budgets focus not just on major categories, but individual components as well. Table 4.6 illustrates an operating budget for our example restaurant. We can use the sales mix targets identified in our sales forecast to separate out individual cost of sales. From the sales mix forecast (Table 4.5), we find mains (55%) and sides and salads (20%) are 75% of total sales. If the restaurant's strategic plan forecasted sales of $520,000, and total cost of sales is 28%, food cost would be budgeted at $520,000 × 28% × 75% = $109,200. Other direct costs are frequently the third-most-important controllable cost. Other direct costs include expenses related to tableware, cleaning, take-out supplies, etc.

All remaining cost items are identified and included in the budget. While there is no required format, these usually fit into one of the following categories: general administration, marketing, rent, utilities and maintenance. Many restaurants will separate controllable from non-controllable

Table 4.6 Annual operating budget

Total revenue					$520,000	100.0%
Food	$109,200	21.0%				
Beverage	$21,840	4.2%				
Liquor	$14,560	2.8%				
Total cost of sales			$145,600	28.0%		
Management labour	$62,400	12.0%				
Variable labour	$91,000	17.5%				
Benefits	$18,200	3.5%				
Total labour			$171,600	33.0%		
Other direct costs			$26,000	5.0%		
Utilities			$18,200	3.5%		
Marketing			$13,000	2.5%		
General administration			$13,000	2.5%		
Maintenance			$7,800	1.5%		
Total controllable cost					$395,200	76.0%
Controllable profit					$124,800	24.0%
Non-controllable cost						
Rent					$93,600	18.0%
Depreciation					$5,000	1.0%
Financing					$2,630	0.5%
Net income before taxes					$23,570	4.5%

expenses. Controllability in accounting refers to the extent to which a particular cost is subject to influence or control by a particular manager.

From Table 4.6, one can assume that the manager did not make the decisions that influenced the restaurant's rent, capital investment and financing because these expense categories are listed within the "Non-Controllable Cost" category. In all likelihood, an owner (or a corporate parent) made the location decision (which determined the rent), a senior manager made capital investment decisions (and accounting made policy choices) that result in depreciation expense, and the accounting and finance departments made choices (i.e. the amount of any loans and interest rates) that impact interest expense. This separation is necessary to properly evaluate a manager's performance – it makes no sense to hold managers accountable for expenditures they cannot control. If all of this sounds familiar: it should; in Chapter 1 you learnt that hotel managers are responsible for anything above, but not below the GOP (gross operating profit) line of an income statement.

Cash budget

A *cash budget* forecasts when cash will be collected and when cash will be paid to others (e.g. for inventory, supplies, labour and utilities). The timing of cash collections and cash disbursements is critical because the restaurant does not want to run out of cash.

For a small, independent restaurant, running out of cash quickly leads to bankruptcy (suppliers usually don't provide supplies on credit to new restaurants). To prevent these cash deficiencies, the restaurant may need to obtain loans. Banks and private lenders will carefully review a restaurant's financial statements.

Cash budgets are typically prepared half-yearly or yearly. Table 4.7 depicts a half-year cash budget in its simplest form. To the beginning cash balance ($2,000), cash collections ($228,750) are added and cash disbursements ($229,016) are subtracted. The ending cash balance will be $1,734. On a cash basis over the six months, it appears the restaurant has lost $266 of its cash. But this does not reveal a serious problem.

Table 4.7 Simple half-year cash budget

Expected beginning balance	$2,000
Add: cash collections	$228,750
Less: disbursements	($229,016)
Expected ending balance	$1,734

Sales are usually paid for in cash or by credit at the time of sale. *Cash sales* result in cash being available immediately. Non-cash sales, known as *credit sales*, likely result in a time lag between when the sale is made and when funds are deposited into the restaurant's bank account. Credit sales create an asset known as *Accounts Receivable* – we hope you remember this balance sheet item from Chapter 2. Banquets, weddings and corporate clients are common sources of credit sales.

Expenses that do not require a cash outlay (e.g. depreciation) are excluded from cash disbursements. Expenses are rarely paid for immediately (suppliers may require cash payment for start-ups without a payment history) as suppliers normally provide goods on credit to continuing customers who they believe will remain an ongoing entity. A common period of credit is for restaurants to be allowed to pay within 30–90 days following the purchase. Where cash is not paid immediately to suppliers, these are called a *credit purchase*. Credit purchases result in the firm recognizing an *Accounts Payable*.

Labour expenditures may also be subject to some delay between incurrence and payment. Employees typically work for one or two weeks prior to being paid. For monthly reporting the overlap is minimal and relatively less so for annual reporting (i.e. by the end of a month, workers have been paid for

Table 4.8 Half-year schedule of cash collections

	January ($)	*February ($)*	*March ($)*	*April ($)*	*May ($)*	*June ($)*
Accounts received 1/1*	7,500					
January sales	24,000	8,000				
February sales		24,000	8,000			
March sales			30,000	10,000		
April sales				27,000	9,000	
May sales					30,000	10,000
June sales						41,250
Total	31,500	32,000	38,000	37,000	39,000	51,250

Closing accounts received 30/6 = $13,750 ($25% × $55,000 June sales)

Note: * Assume the previous month's sales were $30,000.

three weeks of work plus the last week of the prior month so the discrepancy between amounts earned and amounts paid is minor). Utilities (e.g. electricity and water) are sometimes paid quarterly (or may require a one- or two-month deposit) while rent is usually paid monthly.

Preparing the cash budget is complex and firms usually prepare separate schedules of cash collections and cash disbursements. Table 4.8 provides the half-year schedule of cash collections using the hamburger example. The assumptions are: sales volumes are consistent with those given in Figure 4.4; 75% of all sales are cash sales; and 25% of all sales are credit sales. Credit sales are collected in the month following sale and the January 1 accounts receivable balance is $7,500 (i.e. December sales were $30,000).

Table 4.9 shows the half-year schedule of cash disbursements for the year. Assumptions are that one-half of a month's purchases of food, beverage and liquor are paid for in the month of the purchase, while the other half is paid in the following month. As these costs are variable with sales volume, we take the sales each month and multiply by the annual proportion percentages found in Table 4.6. For example, the calculation of April's cost of sales is as follows: April sales × food proportion of sales + April sales × beverage proportion of sales + April sales × liquor's proportion of sales = $36,000 × (21% + 4.2% + 2.8%) = $10,080.

In our cash budget example, wages are paid for in the month they are incurred. Management is usually given a fixed, annual salary. Accordingly, monthly management expense is the annual amount divided by 12 months (i.e. $62,400 / 12 = $5,200).

Variable labour are employees, like cooks and servers, that are paid hourly. In most restaurants, these employees will be sent home early if there are fewer customers than expected or called in early if customer demand is strong. For

Table 4.9 Half-year schedule of cash disbursements

	January ($)	*February ($)*	*March ($)*	*April ($)*	*May ($)*	*June ($)*
Accounts payable 1/1*	4,200					
Cost of sales						
January	4,480	4,480				
February		4,480	4,480			
March			5,600	5,600		
April				5,040	5,040	
May					5,600	5,600
June						7,700
Labour						
January	12,083					
February		12,083				
March			13,649			
April				12,866		
May					13,649	
June						16,586
Miscellaneous	19,500			19,500		
Interest	0	364	364	364	364	364
Rent	7,800	7,800	7,800	7,800	7,800	7,800
Total	48,063	29,207	31,893	51,170	32,453	38,050

Note: *Assume sales the previous month were $30,000, and the same percentages were applied per Table 4.6. This amount was from the December Cost of sales.

this reason, it is common to multiply monthly sales by the annual proportion percentage for variable labour found in Table 4.6. Variable labour for April is calculated as follows: April sales × variable labour proportion of sales = $36,000 × 17.5% = $6,300.

Benefits are a mixed cost. The fixed cost is due to management, whereas the variable cost is related to variable labour. Management labour is $62,400 / ($62,400 + $91,000) = 40.7% of total labour. With annual benefits cost of $18,200, 40.7% ($7,404) is fixed as this is the proportion related to management labour. The remaining amount ($10,796), therefore, is variable. The fixed portion of benefits cost $7,404 is divided by 12 to get a monthly cost of $617. The variable portion ($10,796) is divided by annual sales to calculate its proportion ($10,796 / $520,000 = 2.08%). The cash flow of $1,366 associated with April benefits costs was obtained by summing the fixed ($617) and variable components (April sales × benefits cost variable proportion of sales = $36,000 × 2.08% = $749). Combining these labour expenses, cash flow for labour in April is: $5,200 + $6,300 + $1,366 = $12,866.

For simplicity, other direct costs, utilities, marketing, administration and maintenance are considered fixed costs, and are paid for on the first day of each quarter. In Table 4.9 we label these Miscellaneous. As these are fixed costs, the annual amounts from Table 4.6 are divided by four: ($26,000 + $18,200 + $13,000 + $13,000 + $7,800) / 4 = $19,500). Rent is paid monthly.

After preparing the schedule of cash collections and disbursements, the half-year cash budget (Table 4.10) is prepared.

Management wants to maintain a minimum cash balance of $2,000 and the interest on loans is 20% per annum, paid monthly. Readers will note that cash disbursements will exceed cash collections in the first month (January) by more than $16,000, meaning that the cash balance will be in a deficit without a loan. You might be wondering why restaurant management doesn't take out a loan in January to cover the $16,563 deficiency, leaving the restaurant with its minimum cash balance of $2,000. The reason is that the restaurant would then need a second loan ($5,006) to cover a deficiency in April. So why is the restaurant taking out a larger loan, and why is it incurring interest charges for a larger-than-required loan? The reason is simple: the half-year budget, like the simple analysis (Table 4.7), doesn't reveal problems in the second half of

Table 4.10 Half-year cash budget

	January ($)	*February ($)*	*March ($)*	*April ($)*	*May ($)*	*June ($)*	*Half-Year ($)*
Opening cash balance	2,000	7,270	10,063	16,170	2,000	8,547	2,000
Cash collections	31,500	32,000	38,000	37,000	39,000	51,250	228,750
Less: Disbursements							
Cost of sales	8,680	8,960	10,080	10,640	10,640	13,300	62,300
Labour	12,083	12,083	13,649	12,866	13,649	16,586	80,916
Miscellaneous	19,500	0	0	19,500	0	0	39,000
Rent	7,800	7,800	7,800	7,800	7,800	7,800	46,800
Interest payments	0	364	364	364	364	364	1,819
Total disbursements	48,063	29,207	31,893	51,170	32,453	38,050	230,835
Excess/ (deficiency)	(16,563)	2,793	6,107	(14,170)	6,547	13,200	(2,085)
Loan proceeds	21,833	0	0	0	0	0	21,833
Loan repayments	0	0	0	0	0	0	0
Closing cash balance	7,270	10,063	16,170	2,000	8,547	21,748	21,748

the year. If the restaurant were to repay its loan as early as possible, it would run into cash problems at the end of July, necessitating yet another loan. Each time a firm seeks a loan, management must spend time securing the loan and paying loan origination fees. These fees, plus the "cost" of management time, would likely exceed the monthly interest charges. This example illustrates the importance of preparing the best possible sales forecast, carefully planning its credit sales, working with suppliers to secure credit and arranging financing with individuals, financial institutions, or both. A comprehensive set of budgets will help management ensure the long-term viability of the restaurant. In the next section we see how management uses a budget to identify problems and take corrective actions.

Variance analysis

With a good budget in place, a restaurant manager can now use the accounting system to achieve effective managerial control. By regularly monitoring results, and computing differences relative to the budget, important insights can be gained. The calculation and interpretation of these differences is known as variance analysis.

A *variance* is the difference between an actual and a budgeted amount. It is described as being favourable (F) or unfavourable (U) depending on whether the difference has the effect of increasing or decreasing income, respectively. For example, if a restaurant selling one item (say, hamburgers) budgeted revenues of $1,000,000, but achieved revenues of $1,200,000, the $200,000 difference would be a favourable variance because higher revenues would result in higher income. Similarly, assume a restaurant incurred costs of $700,000, but budgeted costs of $600,000. The restaurant's cost variance would be $100,000 unfavourable because actual costs higher than budgeted costs would, by itself, result in lower income. Variances can be computed for overall income, revenue items, cost items and anything of interest to management (including, for example, quality scores or order processing times). The restaurant's accountant could report actual and budgeted income as shown in Table 4.11.

This analysis is basic and provides no insight; that is, the calculation doesn't explain why a difference exists. The restaurant is making more money, but is it due to higher sales, lower costs, or some combination of the two? Horngren et al. (2006) refer to this analysis as "Level 0". Providing more detail (e.g. as shown in Table 4.12) is helpful.

Table 4.11 Variance analysis – Level 0

Actual income	$500,000
– Budgeted income	$400,000
= Variance	$100,000 F

Table 4.12 Variance analysis – Level 0, expanded

	Budget	*Actual*	*Variance*
Revenue	$1,000,000	$1,200,000	$200,000 F
– Cost	$600,000	$700,000	$100,000 U
= Income	$400,000	$500,000	$100,000 F

Table 4.13 Variance analysis – Level 1

	Budget	*Actual*	*Variance*
Sales volume (covers)	100,000	110,000	10,000 F
Average check	$10.00	$10.91	$0.91 F
Revenue	$1,000,000	$1,200,000	$200,000 F
– Variable cost	$500,000	$575,000	$75,000 U
= Contribution	$500,000	$625,000	$125,000 F
– Fixed cost	$100,000	$125,000	$25,000 U
= Income	$400,000	$500,000	$100,000 F

This report reveals that revenues were higher by $200,000 and, since higher revenues result in higher income, the variance is favourable. If the restaurant could have kept cost at the budgeted amount, restaurant profits would have been $200,000 higher. However, one will quickly realize this expanded analysis still doesn't provide much insight. For example, is the increased revenue the result of higher sales volume (i.e. more covers), higher selling prices (i.e. higher average check), or a combination of both? The increased cost ($100,000 U) may be due to poor cost controls, rising input prices or more. To understand what is going on, restaurant management needs more detail. The report in Table 4.13, known as a Level 1 analysis, provides this detail. The restaurant had greater sales volume (i.e. more covers), a higher average check and higher costs. This new reporting format, called a *contribution margin income statement*, separates costs based on cost behaviour (i.e. fixed and variable). This format helps us recall that variable costs should be higher with higher sales volume.

The problem with Level 1 variances is that these compare financial amounts at two different sales volumes. In short, this is like comparing apples to oranges. The solution is to create a new budget based on the actual output volumes. In other words, "What would restaurant management have budgeted had they known their actual sales volumes?" This new budget is referred to as the *flexible budget* (or, flex budget) and it is an important concept in establishing and understanding variances. The report in Table 4.14 shows this new budget along with new variances.

Table 4.14 Variance analysis – Level 2

	Static budget	*Sales-volume variance*	*Flex budget*	*Flex-budget variance*	*Actual*
Sales volume (covers)	100,000	10,000 F	110,000	0	110,000
Revenue	$1,000,000	$100,000 F	$1,100,000	$100,000 F	$1,200,000
– Variable cost	$500,000	$50,000 U	$550,000	$25,000 U	$575,000
= Contribution	$500,000	$50,000 F	$550,000	$75,000 F	$625,000
– Fixed cost	$100,000	$0	$100,000	$25,000 U	$125,000
= Income	$400,000	$50,000 F	$450,000	$50,000 F	$500,000

This report – a Level 2 analysis – is a big improvement on the prior reports. It is created by adjusting each variable cost to the amount that would be spent at the actual sales volume. For example, we said our restaurant sells just one item: hamburgers. At the static budget of 100,000 units the variable cost was $500,000. This means that the unit variable cost is $5.00 per hamburger. If the manager would have budgeted for 110,000, she would have budgeted a total variable cost of $550,000 (i.e. $5/hamburger × 110,000 hamburgers).[4] Similarly, the sales price was $10/hamburger (obtained by taking total revenue of $1,000,000 divided by 100,000 hamburgers). Assuming price remains constant, the flex budget revenue will be 110,000 hamburgers × $10/hamburger = $1,100,000. Management then budgets what the amount that would have been forecast for fixed cost at the flexible budget volume; in this example, we assumed the increased sales volume was within the relevant range and the flexible budget fixed cost was simply equal to the static budget fixed cost.

With the flexible budget completed, note that there are now two sets of variances: *sales-volume variances* and *flexible-budget variances*. The former are due solely to changes in sales volume, whereas the latter are meaningful because they represent differences between what should have been accomplished at the actual level of sales volume and the actual results. Focusing on the sales-volume variances, note that sales volume increased by 10,000 covers. This would result in $100,000 greater revenue and $50,000 greater variable cost. The fixed cost doesn't change unless the sales volume change is sufficient to warrant a change in the restaurant's fixed costs. The reason for the sales volume change is due to differences in the market size, the restaurant's market share or, in the case of multi-product firms, the sales mix. These differences will be explained later.

From the flexible-budget variances, you can see that the restaurant achieved higher-than-expected revenues. This is due solely to the restaurant achieving a higher average sales price on its hamburgers. You can see that the restaurant's actual variable cost is $25,000 higher than the flexible budget amount and the actual fixed cost is $25,000 higher than expected (i.e. the flexible budget amount). From this table, it is obvious that the firm could have earned another $50,000 in profit had costs been managed to expectations.

At this point, the astute reader might realize there is another level of analysis. What remains to be done is to understand the reason for the $25,000 unfavourable flexible budget variance. First, let's assume the variable cost consists entirely of direct materials and, for purposes of illustration, that there is one ingredient (hamburger beef). That is, let's pretend that the buns, condiments (i.e. pickles, lettuce, etc.) are free and that there is no labour cost. The flexible budget variable cost results from the static budget's variable cost per unit ($10/pound) times the standard amount of beef (i.e. 1/2 pound/burger). That is, total standard cost is the standard amount of material *per* hamburger (i.e. 1/2 pound/burger) times the standard cost *per* burger (i.e. $10/pound × 1/2 pound/burger = $5/burger). If the restaurant were to prepare 110,000 burgers, the total flexible budget cost would be 110,000 burgers × $5/burger = $550,000. The actual variable cost is the result of the price paid (i.e. actual price) times the amount of beef actually purchased. Assume the restaurant paid $9.75/pound for the beef. Since it spent $575,000, this means the restaurant must have received $575,000/$9.75/pound = 58,974.359 pounds of beef.

The Level 3 variance ($25,000 U) comes about for one of two possible reasons: either the price paid differs from our expected amount, or the amount of material differs from the expected amount. We begin with the former. If we want to estimate the total financial impact (e.g. in dollars [$]) of a price change, one would begin with looking at the difference in prices: Actual price minus Standard price (i.e. AP – SP). For the example here, that is $10/pound minus $9.75/pound = $0.25/pound. The reader will notice that we want the total impact (in $) and the price difference is the impact *per pound*. Accordingly, we must multiply the price difference by the amount of beef purchased (in pounds). The total variance is $0.25/pound × 58,974.359 pounds = $14,743.59. Since the lower price of beef would have the effect – all else equal – of increasing profit, the variance is favourable. The managerial accountant reports a direct material *price variance* as $14,743.59 F.

We now turn to the other possible reason: a difference in the amount of material used. Since each burger is 1/2 pound, selling 110,000 burgers should result in the consumption of 55,000 pounds of beef (i.e. 110,000 burgers × 0.5 pound/burger). The difference in the quantity of material used is 58,974.359 pounds – 55,000 pounds = 3,974.359 pounds. To get the financial impact of the quantity variation, multiply this difference by the standard (i.e. expected) price. The variance is then $39,743.59 (3,974.359 pounds × $10/pound). Since the restaurant used more beef than expected, this would have the effect – again, all else equal – of lowering profits and so the variance is unfavourable. The accountant reports the direct material *quantity variance* as $39,743.59 U.

Summed together, the direct material price variance ($14,743.59 F) and direct material quantity variance ($39,743.59 U) is $25,000 U, the Level 2 variance. While this chapter's example assumed only one direct material item and no labour, it is a simple matter to extend variance calculations for each item of direct material, and for direct labour. Further, it is a simple matter to extend analysis to include multiple products. The calculations are not difficult, but they are tedious. Spreadsheets make the process fast and error-free. In large organisations, accounting software can be programmed to produce reports since the information is already contained in the accounting system.

As mentioned above, the sales volume variances arise from volume changes due to differences in the market size, the restaurant's market share or, in the case of multi-product firms, the sales mix. The *sales mix* is the proportion of sales volume that is associated with each product sold. In the examples so far, we have assumed a single product – hamburgers. Assume now that the restaurant has both hamburgers and salads, and management budgeted the data shown in Table 4.15.

Lastly, assume that the restaurant sold 53,000 hamburgers and 57,000 salads. This would result in the data provided in Table 4.16.

Let's assume the manager created the static budget based on a forecasted market size of 1,000,000 covers and a market share of 10% (i.e. 1,000,000 × 0.1 = 100,000 covers). At the end of the year, the manager estimated the actual market size to be 1,200,000 covers. At the end of the year, market data enable the manager to create two additional flexible budgets: (1) One using

Table 4.15 Budgeted data, hamburgers and salads

	Hamburgers	*Salads*
Quantity	50,000	50,000
Unit sales price	$10	$8
Unit variable cost	$5	$4

Table 4.16 Sales-volume variances

	Static budget	*Sales-volume variance*	*Flex budget*
Sales volume (covers)	100,000	10,000 F	110,000
Revenue	$900,000	$86,000 F	$986,000
– Variable cost	$450,000	$43,000 U	$493,000
= Contribution	$450,000	$43,000 F	$493,000
– Fixed cost	$100,000	$0	$100,000
= Income	$350,000	$43,000 F	$393,000

Table 4.17 Revenue variances

	Static budget	*Flex-1 budget*	*Flex-2 budget*	*Flex budget*
Market size	S	A	A	A
Market share	S	S	A	A
Sales mix	S	S	S	A
Sales volume (covers)	100,000	120,000	110,000	110,000
Revenue	$900,000	$1,080,000	$990,000	$986,000
– Variable cost	450,000	540,000	495,000	493,000
= Contribution	$450,000	$540,000	$495,000	$493,000
– Fixed cost	100,000	100,000	100,000	100,000
= Income	$350,000	$440,000	$395,000	$393,000
	$90,000 F	$45,000 U	$2,000 U	
	Market Size	Market Share	Sales Mix	

estimated actual market size and budgeted market share, sales mix, prices and costs (Flex-1); and, (2) one using actual market size and actual market share (i.e. the restaurant's sales volume of 53,000 hamburgers and 57,000 salads) (Flex-2), while maintaining standard sales mix, prices and costs. Note that the original flexible budget uses the actual market size, actual market share and actual sales mix. The resulting *revenue variances* are shown in Table 4.17.

The three headers (*Market size, Market share* and *Sales mix*) remind readers how each budget was prepared – S indicates "Standard" and "A" represents "Actual". Note that the only difference between the Static Budget and Flex-1 Budget is that the market size has changed from "S" to "A" as the market grew from 1.0 million to 1.2 million covers. The impact of that change, if everything else had been unchanged (i.e. at "S"), is a $90,000 increase in income. The market size variance is, therefore, $90,000 F. Comparing Flex-1 and Flex-2, the reader will realize the income decrease of $45,000 is due solely to the change in market share, this difference being *after* the market size has been taken into account. Finally, note that the only difference between Flex-2 and the Flex Budget is the change in sales mix, the result being a $2,000 unfavourable sales mix variance.

As we began this section trying to understand why actual results differed from the budget, readers might not realize that the purpose of variance analysis is to understand performance. Accordingly, variance analysis should not be used to assign blame. Approaching analysis in this way is a sure way to get employees to "pad" budgets and look for excuses. Managers should ask who in the organisation might be able to explain variance. For example, an unfavourable efficiency variance might be the result of quality problems resulting from the purchase of low-quality raw materials. These low-quality materials might have been purchased at a lower price, resulting in a favourable materials price variance. A carefully-prepared budget with realistic expectations, combined with variance analysis, is the foundation for effective managerial control. That is, these tools make possible the modern organisation. Without them, fraud and inefficiency by non-owner managers would soon bankrupt an organisation.

Conclusion

Restaurant managers must know how to plan ahead and then later exercise control so as to ensure that their establishments perform well. The first step is to determine which costs are fixed, variable or mixed over a given time period. For example, rent might be fixed in the short-term but variable in the long-term. Knowing how these costs behave is essential to developing operating and cash budgets. A sales forecast is necessary for the purpose of budgeting, variable costs will vary in direct proportion to the predicted sales, whereas fixed costs will remain constant with changes in sales volume, while mixed costs exhibit some combination of these. After the budgets are prepared and the restaurant has conducted business for the period covered by the budget, managers can learn a great deal by exercising control through the conduct of various variance analyses. By enacting the techniques of planning and control outlined in this chapter restaurant managers can ensure a more professional dispensation of their duties; improving the restaurant's performance.

Reference

Horngren, C. T., Datar, S. M. and Foster, G. (2006). *Cost Accounting: A Managerial Emphasis*, 12th edn. Upper Saddle River, NJ: Pearson.

PRACTICE: DIARY OF AN EXECUTIVE CHEF

Michael Dutnall

Note to the reader: this "diary" was written in 2018. For this second edition, Chef Dutnall has been kind enough to add a short "epilogue" at the end, highlighting how the challenges of being an executive chef have changed quite a bit since then.

As you will appreciate after having studied the theory section of this chapter, operating a commercial kitchen profitably requires insight into various financial measures, such as food cost of sales, payroll costs and the costs of equipment. This practice section explains a number of financial reports available to chefs and provides thought on how to react to the information these reports provide. In addition, practical advice is shared on how to best manage the financial health of a kitchen by combining information from both internal and external sources and making sound managerial decisions at the right time to ensure profitability percentages are achieved in line with the budget and forecast of the business.

Introduction

The Royal Air Force Club in Mayfair, London is a private members' club that welcomes current and former officers of the Royal Air Force and their direct family. As it is a not-for-profit organisation, all revenue from the five-star quality offerings its 24,000 members enjoy is reinvested in the club and its Grade II listed building in Central London. Next to its 110 bedrooms, the RAF Club is renowned for its high-quality food and beverage services and to our members is a home away from home. It houses the Running Horse Tavern, the Cowdray Lounge and a wonderful Dining Room where it serves à la carte dishes for breakfast, lunch and dinner. In addition, the eight function rooms including the Library and the Ballroom are the backdrop of many private and club events ranging from weddings to gourmet dinners.

As Executive Chef of the RAF Club, I manage the financial health of the kitchens that provide food for the various outlets and events in the Club. Our brigade consists of 23 chefs and seven kitchen porters. There are certain recurring financial checkpoints and safety nets which help me manage the expenses of my department, e.g. the *food flash* and the daily revenue report. Any kitchen has various financial aspects that all need to be aligned in order to achieve healthy profitability: payroll, food purchasing and all the products needed to run the kitchen (including everything from piping bags to cleaning supplies to frying pans). I will take you through two weeks of my working cycle to give you an example of a kitchen's financial management process.

Daily information and key measurements

Food flash

On a daily basis I receive the food flash from our Cost Controller, an example of which is pictured in Figure 4.3. It shows the revenue generated by meal period and outlet. It also specifies how much revenue was made through functions in our meeting rooms and events hosted by the Club for which we charge an entry/participation fee. It then shows the total value of the food purchases received per day. On a weekly basis, we divide the total food purchases by the total F&B revenue which gives us the *food cost*.

This is one of the most important key performance indicators (KPIs) in a kitchen. The target food cost a chef works towards differs depending on what type of establishment they work in. Typically, it can vary from 20% to 30%. In general, fine dining restaurants work on the higher end of the spectrum whereas fast food businesses would be around the lowest mark. The target in our Club is 30%. In a kitchen operation, food cost is such an important measurement that it is not uncommon for a Chef's bonuses to be linked to the budgeted percentage being achieved.

	01-Feb	02-Feb	03-Feb	04-Feb	05-Feb	06-Feb	07-Feb
Breakfast	983.13	991.25	793.33	850.63	268.13	520	544.38
Restaurant lunch	257.08	187.88	165	804.16	311.83	535.83	540.33
Restaurant dinner	671.07	722.91	693.88	224.75	0	811.37	751.77
Cowdry day time	40.83	9.88	21.83	10.5	31.83	37.13	83.63
Cowdray evening	115.50	446.5	255.21	160.46	79.83	131.33	141.96
Running Horse lunch	96.67	85.29	261.67	128.67	46.92	290.17	159.38
Running Horse dinner	120.42	225.9	70.73	203.58	175.53	253.83	96.11
Functions	3,450	5,288.34	7,795	900.83	389.17	3,882.92	4,774.58
Events	0.00	0	0	0	300	1,045.33	0
Total revenue	5,734.70	7,957.95	10,056.65	3,283.58	1,603.24	7,507.91	7,092.14
Total food cost	3,754.91	1,316.90	1,225.62	82.70	2,591.28	2,833.26	1,192.90
Average cost (month to date)							25.20%

Figure 4.3 Food flash

It is not overly helpful to look at food cost on a daily basis, as the food received on a day is usually not served on the same day. Therefore, we look at the figures for the week, fortnight and month. In the UK, hot beverages and fruit juices are also considered food and are therefore included in food cost and food revenue numbers.

It is important to check these documents daily to spot any mistakes. For example, we run hosted Club events with guest speakers for around 100 attendees. These events usually include a three-course meal. Tickets are sold and paid for in advance, which means the money has already been received by the Club a few days prior to the event. If we then fail to allocate this money (revenue) to the various departments involved and do not split the ticket price into food revenue, beverage revenue and meeting room revenue, there will be no food revenue visible in the "Events" line in the food flash, even though the costs of the food we have bought in for this event are visible. This would show our food cost in a much more negative light than it actually is.

Daily revenue report

In addition to the food flash, our Finance team sends out the daily revenue report. The daily revenue report is a snapshot of the business' total performance of the previous day and month to date giving both the Rooms and Food and Beverage departments insight into their performance. For Rooms, it shows occupancy percentage (96.55% in the below), average rate per room (£111.42), total rooms revenue (£9,359), etc. For F&B, it includes how many guests dined (our *covers*) during which meal period (breakfast, lunch or dinner) in each different food outlet, the total income for all outlets on the day and the average spend or average check per cover.

Supplier information

Apart from the information supplied by the Club, a number of my food suppliers send out daily specials. In my case, those are my meat supplier and fish supplier. It shows which products I can purchase for good value. These products can then be used for daily or weekly specials, or served in the staff restaurant. The lower the costs of the ingredients in a dish, the lower the food cost will turn out.

Next to the information I get sent, I also actively go out looking for updated booking numbers in our reservation system and liaise with the Events team to get final numbers for the events in the upcoming days. Any variance in numbers can have a direct impact on your food cost: for example, an event in two days' time that was for 100 covers has dropped to 80 covers. Most likely, the food for this will already have been ordered so it leaves me with 20 portions of entrecote steaks that I now need to use somewhere else to avoid them from going to waste. The daily routine in the kitchen also includes checking the

TODAYS DATE	22-03-2018									
	Thursday 22 Mar 2018					March 2018				
	TODAY - LY Wed					MONTH TO DATE				
STATISTICS	**Actual**	**Budget**	**Var £**	**Last Year**	**Var £**	**Actual**	**Budget**	**Var £**	**Last Year**	**Var £**
Rooms Occupied	84	78	6	87	-3	1,575	1,723	-148	1,678	-103
Rooms Available	87	89	-2	87	0	1,914	1,958	-44	1,914	0
Occupancy	96.55%	88.00%	8.55%	100.00%	-0	82.29%	88.00%	-5.71%	82.45%	-0.16%
Average Room Rate	£111.42	£107.00	£4.42	£107.97	£3.45	£112.30	£107.00	£5.30	£100.43	£11.88
REVPar	£107.58	£94.16	£13.45	£107.97	£0.39	£92.41	£94.16	-£1.75	£82.80	£9.61
Complimentary Rooms	-	0	0	1	-1	13	-	13	14	-1
Out of order	8	4	2	6	0	148	79	69	152	-4
NO SHOWS	-	0	0	0	0	26	-	26	12	14
Sleepers (Beds let)	130	119	11	119	11	2,315	2,619	-304	2,480	-165
INCOME										
Rooms income	9,359	8,380	979	9,393	-34	176,876	184,365	-7,489	175,734	1,142
Breakfast	778	621	157	514	264	13,125	13,672	-547	12,352	773
Dining Room	3,075	1,824	1,252	1,702	1,373	38,942	40,117	-1,176	39,362	-420
Cowdray Lounge	1,546	690	856	560	987	15,163	15,187	-24	15,796	-633
Running Horse	1,434	1,054	380	1,192	242	22,990	23,192	-202	22,379	611
Nigh/Recep	0	0	0	8	-8	0	0	0	30	-30
Subtotal - Bars & Dining Rooms	6,834	4,189	2,644	3,977	2,857	90,220	92,169	-1,949	89,919	301
Functions & Events	10,993	6,203	4,790	9,823	1,170	152,814	136,471	16,343	136,733	16,082
F&B Total	17,827	10,393	7,434	13,799	4,027	243,034	228,640	14,395	226,652	16,382
Other	19	145	-126	20	-1	390	3,194	-2,804	4,021	-3,631
Shop	171	97	74	-42	212	6,932	2,129	4,803	1,395	5,537
Total Income	27,376	19,015	8,361	23,171	4,205	427,232	418,327	8,905	407,802	19,431
COVERS	**Actual**	**Budget**	**Var £**	**Last Year**	**Var £**	**Actual**	**Budget**	**Var £**	**Last Year**	**Var £**
Breakfast Covers	83	79	4	70	13	1,562	1,742	-180	1,578	-16
Breakfast Ave Check	£9.37	£7.85	£1.51	£7.35	£2.03	£8.40	£7.85	£0.55	£7.83	£0.58
Capture Rate	63.85%	66.50%	-2.65%	58.82%	5.02%	67.47%	66.50%	0.97%	63.63%	3.84%
Dining Room Covers	100	64	36	59	41	1,245	1,405	-160	1,406	-161
Dining Room Ave Check	£30.75	£28.55	£2.20	£28.85	£1.90	£31.28	£28.55	£2.73	£28.00	£3.28
R/Horse Checks	180	139	41	169	11	3,010	3,052	-42	3,044	-34
R/Horse Ave Check	£7.97	£7.60	£0.37	£7.05	£0.91	£7.64	£7.60	£0.04	£7.35	£0.29
Functions - Events Cvrs	126	135	-9	180	-54	3,555	2,981	574	3,053	502
Functions - Events Ave Check	£87.25	£45.79	£41.46	£54.57	£32.68	£42.99	£45.79	-£2.80	£44.79	-£1.80
Cowdray Checks	174	129	45	123	51	2,745	2,839	-94	3,032	-287
Cowdray Ave Check	£8.89	£5.53	£3.54	£4.55	£4.34	£5.52	£5.35	£0.17	£5.21	£0.31

Figure 4.4 Daily revenue report

fridges holding high value items such as meat and fish to ensure they are still within shelf life. Any food spoilage is not only an unnecessary waste, it will also have an impact on the department's food cost as it is money spent without any money made from it.

Mid-month report

Around the fifteenth day of the month, finance teams in large companies can send out mid-month figures. These reports usually show revenues vs. budget, a comparison to last year and an overview of the performance of each department and outlet. It can also specify the costs that have been made so far to keep the department running – in that case, it is basically an "interim" profit and loss statement (P&L) with roughly the same information as the P&L at the end of the month would include. As our Club is not a massive company,

	16 Feb	*17 Feb*	*18 Feb*
Breakfast	651.46	706.46	756.04
Restaurant lunch	886.96	367.67	740.42
Restaurant dinner	1,121.63	1,084.01	840.67
Cowdray day time	29.42	46.25	8.83
Cowdray evening	357.98	351.21	431.5
Running Horse lunch	290.13	318.29	122.71
Running Horse dinner	405.11	354.4	155.18
Functions	2,175.42	2,794.16	665.83
Events	83.33	0	0
Total revenue	**6,001.44**	**6,022.45**	**3,721.18**
Total food cost	**4,447.81**	**1,086.78**	**90.29**
Average cost (month to date)	-	-	**30.23%**

Figure 4.5 Mid-month report

I usually use the daily revenue report and a food flash of a day mid-way through the month and look at the month to date figures to have a sense-check of how we are doing so far. In the example below, we are slightly too high in terms of food cost – 30.32% instead of the goal of 30%.

Food cost may be of vital importance to the management of the kitchen, but it is not the only financial target we look at. In addition to food cost, payroll is a big expense for any kitchen operation – as it is for the entire hospitality industry. The costs of payroll could make up to 50% of the total costs of running a kitchen and therefore it is extremely important that these costs are controlled in a sensible way. The third significant chunk of costs of operating a kitchen is the money spent on all products used to operate the kitchen – i.e. what we need to cook and produce the dishes. This ranges from cling film to date labels to whisks to mixing jugs. We will look at both of these sets of costs in a bit more detail later on.

Managing of costs in response to mid-month

In the mid-month report above, our food cost is slightly higher than we would like it to be, with 0.23% above our target. It is then up to me as Executive Chef to work with my team to ensure this is brought down to show a healthy figure at the end of the month.

Food cost variances: how to identify and mitigate

From the daily information I received throughout the month, I am aware of a number of contributing factors that have pushed up the food cost. First of all, the costs of some of our ingredients skyrocketed. Egg prices are still up as a result of the recent fipronil crisis in mainland Europe. An algae disease killed large numbers of fish driving up the price of e.g. salmon, which is a popular ingredient in restaurants. The announcement of Brexit made the British Pound significantly drop in value, making it more beneficial for British farmers to export their goods to other European countries, leading to fewer products being available for the businesses in Britain. More recently, the unusually bad weather in the first quarter of 2018 prevented many fishermen from going out, which meant the supply of fish dropped and prices which are driven by demand increased. To ensure the impact of these developments is limited I would then re-look at my menus and make alternative choices for our weekly menus and event menus. We have a database of suppliers that we work with, so just as people would use various supermarkets to keep the costs of their own weekly shop down, we also check which supplier has the best deals available.

Before changing the menus, there are a number of other things I can do or check to firstly ensure the food cost displayed is the correct figure, and secondly bring it back down to healthy levels. To verify the food cost is correct, I check back on a number of invoices received and compare them to our orders. If the supplier is either charging more for products than were actually delivered, or a higher price per product than what was agreed, the food cost turns out higher than it should be. This does not mean that our suppliers are trying to trick us, but could for example happen if a price change has not been uploaded into their invoicing system yet. As we work with fresh produce, it can happen that a delivery that comes in is sent back due to quality issues; a batch of pigeons were delivered recently but were already too old to meet our quality standards. This produce is then rejected and returned to the supplier. They would normally issue a *credit note* (which is essentially a refund to the Club) however most suppliers only issue credit notes at the end of the month. Until the refund is received, the costs of these pigeons will be sitting in our food cost, elevating it temporarily. Another mistake that can occur in food invoicing is a difference in weight specifications: when ordering fish, it is quite common to order either based on "whole weight" (the weight of not only the piece of fish that will be used, but also wasted areas such as head and bones) or "filleted weight", which only includes useable areas of the fish. If I order 10kg of salmon, the whole weight price per kg may be £6, whereas the filleted weight price per kg could be £12. If an invoice then comes in showing the price for 10kg of filleted salmon whereas actually we received 10kg of salmon whole weight, this needs to be rectified to ensure it is accurate and does not negatively impact the food cost.

The mistake could also be on the Club's side. Next to the meals we prepare for our members, we cater for our staff for breakfast, lunch and dinner every day. To give an indication of the costs involved in looking after our teams, the pure food cost of staff meals for a month would be around £5,500. This may seem like a big chunk of money, but when discounted to a per person rate, it means that the kitchen has roughly £1.80 to spend per day for a team member. It would be a challenge for any of our staff to find a decent lunch for that money in Central London. All costs for staff food need to be transferred out to the separate department, or in financial terms *cost centre*, Staff Feeding. If this is not done correctly, the food cost will be showing very high percentages as the costs of all food bought in for staff would be included, but there would be no revenue generated from it as it is a free benefit for the teams. Similarly, there are other staff appreciation activities such as parties for which the Human Resources department requests food or snacks from the kitchen. If the costs for this food are then not internally transferred to the Human Resources department, the food cost will be unfairly high.

As mentioned earlier, it is important to limit food spoilage and wastage in the kitchen as this negatively impacts the food cost. At times, there may be incidents that lead to wastage that cannot be prevented. Earlier in the month, one of our freezers malfunctioned and a number of tubs of ice cream melted. Unfortunately, this cost will stay and drive up the food cost for this month. It is important to be aware of these kinds of events impacting food cost as during monthly P&L meetings the Financial Controller may ask you to clarify financial results. Despite our best efforts to manage our costs, there will always be surprises along the way that we have to react to. For example, an event with 100 guests that did not highlight any dietary requirements prior to arrival could turn out to have five vegetarians in attendance on the night. This means that we will have five pieces of meat that may have already been cooked but cannot be served. Not only do we then have to take the hit on wastage of these items, we also have to spend additional money as we have to prepare vegetarian dishes for these five guests.

Every kitchen is different and no month is the same, so there can be many other causes of an elevated food cost apart from the ones mentioned above. To limit the risk, it is good practice to regularly check invoices, keep an eye on market price fluctuations (especially for expensive items such as meat and fish) and always be aware of your stock levels to avoid wastage and use any superfluous stock elsewhere. Next to checking invoices coming in to ensure the amounts charged are correct, it is also important to check that all invoices received are paid for promptly – if they are not, the costs will hit the kitchen in a later month. It is not an exact science, but a professional manager is expected not to deviate more than 3% from his targeted food cost. If larger variances happen, they would normally have to be explained to stakeholders such as owners, senior leadership and financial controllers.

A food cost percentage significantly *lower* than budget may seem like a great achievement, but actually it is usually an indication that something is not quite right; a number of things may have gone wrong to have led to a lower than expected food cost. As the end of the month (in financial terms: *month end*) approaches, departmental managers are asked to submit their *accruals*. An accrual is an amount of money that has been spent, but for which the Club has not been invoiced yet. For example, an order of 80 fillet steaks could be worth roughly £650. If that order was placed on 28 March, delivered on the 30 and served on the 31, then financially this money was spent in March and the revenue was made in March. The invoice may only come in a week later, which would be 7 April. To ensure our financial figures for the month are accurate, we need to inform the finance team to "accrue" these £650 and include them in the March costs even though we have not actually paid the invoice yet. If the accruals are not done correctly, then certain costs are shown in the wrong month which skews the figures and may lead to a very nice and low food cost in March. It would then hit in April though, leading to an elevated food cost in that month. In a professional work environment, once your month end figures have been published, there is no adjusting them. In our example this would mean that April starts off very negatively with £650 of costs for which we do not have any revenue in that month – not a situation I want to be in.

In an establishment of the quality of the RAF Club, our members expect products and offerings of a superior quality. Technically, I could drive my food cost down by using lower quality ingredients or by moving away from fresh produce and replacing it with cheaper alternatives such as tinned or frozen items. This would however have a detrimental effect in the long term, as it would impact the quality of the dishes we offer and most likely will not get the same level of appreciation from our members. If the satisfaction of our members drops, there is a risk they may not return for another visit or will share negative feedback which will hurt the reputation of the Club and its future potential. Again, a low food cost could also have to do with incorrect administration – e.g. if an event is posted twice and therefore an evening would be reported as having 100 guests even though there were only 50, it will seem as if we managed to cook for 100 whilst only buying items for 50, which will skew the percentage and make it look falsely positive.

Month end

In any professional hospitality business, financial results are published on a monthly basis in what is called a *month end report*. The month end report analyses in detail what the financial performance was for the month just passed. Usually, a month end report gets published between the fifth and tenth day of the new month, though different businesses have different deadlines in place for the Finance team to produce these reports. As mentioned above, as a head of department some responsibility lies with you to supply the Finance team with the correct information as to which costs to accrue and therefore include in the month before closing the month. The month end reports are usually discussed by the management team in an HOD (heads of department) meeting or a separate P&L meeting.

Kitchen results in month end report

Next to food cost which we have discussed in length above, there are a number of measurements in the department's month end report that need to be checked and analysed. In any service business, payroll takes up a significant if not the highest percentage of costs to operate the business. For our kitchen team, there are two main segments within the payroll costs. Firstly, there is a group of chefs on our *fixed* payroll – they have an employment contract with the Club and get a monthly salary depending on their level and job title. In our Club, all Sous Chefs, Chef de Parties, Demi Chef de Parties etc. are contracted and their salaries would be reflected in the "main kitch. total salaries" line in our month end report. Next to our fixed payroll, we spend money on contracted labour, which is the cost of agency chefs who come in for certain shifts to help the team. We pay an agency for the work of these chefs per hour and the agency in turn pays the chefs. In addition, some of our kitchen porters who look after washing all the dishes and cleaning the kitchen work through an agency and are therefore paid per hour.

Rather than focusing on one specific number, it is always important to look at how one specific result compares to other indicators and draw conclusions from the overall picture. For example, the month end report shows that the kitchen has overspent £2,270 on agency staff costs. Looking at that figure alone would lead one to believe that payroll was not managed correctly. However, when taking into consideration other numbers, it comes to light that a lot less costs were made in terms of fixed payroll cost, as the main kitchen total salaries are £6,603 down vs. budget: for example, this could happen when we have a vacancy for a full-time Chef and need to cover this role with agency chefs temporarily.

A set of costs related to payroll are employee benefits. In terms of money, a very important chunk of employee benefits is the paid holiday days that they are entitled to. Even though a team member does not work, his/her salary is still a cost to us during their holidays as they get paid for their holidays. Some businesses include the costs for holidays in the normal salaries line, whereas others reflect it separately in a line for employee benefits or holidays. It is important that holidays are managed correctly and spread out over the year in periods where workload is relatively light. If this is not done correctly and holidays are approved for busy periods or too many holidays are approved at the same time, this will negatively impact your monthly results. Apart from paying for the holidays of the fixed payroll chefs, there will be additional charges for the agency chefs who need to be called in to cover the shifts.

Some companies in the UK pay their employees when they are unwell, which is called sick pay. Sick pay would be another employee benefit that has a cost attached to it for the company, and may in addition require spending money on agency chefs to cover the work of the chef who is off ill. Benefits vary per company and there may be many others visible on a month end report, such as dry cleaning, medical insurance or taxis to bring staff home after a late shift.

Rather than looking at the costs of payroll as a whole amount, payroll is usually measured as a percentage of departmental revenue. Many managers in the industry would have the payroll percentage as a performance target. In our month end report, we look at payroll as a percentage of food revenue.

The last main group of costs contains the expenses we make for the equipment and materials used in the kitchen. On a financial report, these are usually spread over various cost centres such as e.g. stationary (printing paper, till rolls), cleaning supplies, disposables (cling film, blue roll, piping bags, rubber gloves, baking paper), utensils (chopping boards, measuring jugs, pans) and small kitchen equipment (blenders, meat slicers). We also record any costs for the repairs of any equipment that needs servicing (usually large items such as fridges or ovens) and the upkeep of our equipment. Costs for upkeep would for example include regular cleaning of our hoods and extract vents – which is a legal requirement in the UK. Generally, any equipment of higher value than the items in small kitchen equipment would be reported separately from the monthly finances as they are expected to last multiple years. These are items such as ovens, fryers, fridges, etc. and they are usually classed as CapEx (Capital Expenditure) items.

The month end report typically starts with a summary overview of all revenues made in the month, followed by a summary of all costs incurred in the month.

Royal Air Force Club Kitchen - 212
April 2018

	CURRENT MONTH							YEAR TO DATE						
	Actual	Budget	Var £	%	Last Year	Var £	%	Actual	Budget	Var £	%	Last Year	Var £	%
REVENUE														
Rooms Revenue	230,973	234,907	-3,934	-2%	222,461	8,511	4%	898,877	911,908	-13,030	-1%	852,454	46,423	5%
Food Revenue	176,947	180,753	-3,807	-2%	171,903	5,044	3%	699,511	655,713	43,798	7%	628,267	71,244	11%
Total Room & Food Revenue	**407,919**	**415,660**	-7,741	**-2%**	**394,364**	13,555	**3%**	**1,598,388**	**1,567,621**	30,767	**2%**	**1,480,721**	117,667	**8%**
PAYROLL														
Main Kit. Total Salaries	43,863	50,466	-6,603	-13%	28,197	15,665	56%	172,756	181,703	-8,947	-5%	118,535	54,221	46%
Main Kit. Zero Hours	0	0	0		2,420	-2,420		307	0	307	0%	7,754	-7,447	-96%
Main Kit. Agency Staff	2,270	0	2,270	0%	4,622	-2,352	-51%	2,802	0	2,802	0%	8,450	-5,648	-67%
Main Kit. Otime/Extra Pay	342	0	342	0%	118	224	189%	541	0	541	0%	690	-149	-22%
Main Kit. Bonus Provision	2,911	3,064	-153	-5%	2,265	646	29%	11,643	12,256	-613	-5%	9,059	2,584	29%
Main Kit. Pension 12%	1,778	2,225	-447	-20%	1,500	279	19%	6,612	8,901	-2,290	-26%	6,245	367	6%
Main Kit. Pension 8%	0	0	0		0	0		0	0	0		0	0	
Main Kit. Pension 5%	0	0	0		0	0		0	0	0		0	0	
Main Kit. Group/Spouse	10	35	-25	-71%	34	-23	-69%	41	140	-99	-71%	135	-93	-69%
Main Kit. PHI	20	75	-55	-74%	75	-55	-74%	78	300	-222	-74%	300	-222	-74%
Main Kit. Pension Admin	0	0	0		0	0		0	0	0		0	0	
Main Kit. Sick Pay	0	0	0		0	0		0	0	0		88	-88	
Main Kit. Staff Party	134	0	134	0%	0	134	0%	484	0	484	0%	0	484	0%
Main Kit. Employers N.I.	4,267	5,297	-1,030	-19%	3,065	1,202	39%	17,326	19,272	-1,946	-10%	12,839	4,488	35%
Main Kit. StaffLaund/Dry Clng	142	175	-33	-19%	145	-3	-2%	556	700	-144	-21%	532	24	4%
Main Kit. Med.Ins.	87	78	9	11%	78	9	11%	316	314	2	1%	252	64	25%
Main Kit. Advertising	0	0	0		0	0		700	0	700	0%	0	700	0%
Main Kit. Agency Recruit Fees	0	0	0		0	0		0	0	0		0	0	
Main Kit. Staff Taxi Journeys	0	0	0		12	-12		612	0	612	0%	27	585	2,143%
Main Kit. Educational Trips	0	0	0		0	0		0	0	0		0	0	
Main Kit. (B/D) Training	0	0	0		0	0		375	0	375	0%	230	145	63%
Main Kit. First Aid	0	0	0		0	0		0	0	0		0	0	
Main Kit. Canteen Charges	1,682	2,242	-560	-25%	1,909	-227	-12%	7,099	8,859	-1,760	-20%	7,213	-114	-2%
Main Kit. Miscellaneous	0	0	0		29	-29		0	0	0		29	-29	
Main Kit. Personnel Costs	0	0	0		519	-519		0	0	0		1,589	-1,589	
Main Kit Payroll Costs	**57,506**	**63,657**	-6,151	**-10%**	**44,988**	12,518	**28%**	**222,249**	**232,445**	-10,196	**-4%**	**173,967**	48,282	**28%**
As a % of FOOD Revenue	**32.50%**	**35.22%**			**26.17%**			**31.77%**	**35.45%**			**27.69%**		

Figure 4.6 Month end report

EXPENSES														
Main Kit. Clng.Supplies	1,849	1,754	95	5%	1,754	95	5%	6,263	6,629	-366	-6%	6,629	-366	-6%
Main Kit. Telephone Calls	24	0	24	0%	15	8	54%	87	0	87	0%	63	24	38%
Main Kit. Printing & Staionery	342	189	153	81%	189	153	81%	465	346	118	34%	346	118	34%
Main Kit. Utensils	321	39	282	724%	39	282	724%	680	1,184	-504	-43%	1,184	-504	-43%
Main Kit. Misc.Op.Costs	647	0	647	0%	0	647	0%	772	123	649	527%	123	649	527%
Main Kit. China	0	0	0		0	0		542	279	263	94%	279	263	94%
Main Kit. Linen	0	0	0		0	0		0	0	0		0	0	
Main Kit. Uniforms	1,326	1,045	281	27%	1,045	281	27%	6,941	4,692	2,249	48%	4,692	2,249	48%
Main Kit. Contract Clng.	0	0	0		0	0		0	0	0		0	0	
Main Kit. Dept Laundry	0	0	0		0	0		0	0	0		0	0	
Main Kit.Dept Dry Clng	0	0	0		0	0		0	0	0		0	0	
Main Kit. Laundry Trfr.	479	232	247	107%	233	246	106%	1,579	927	652	70%	736	843	115%
Main Kit. Squirrel Costs	0	0	0		0	0		0	0	0		0	0	
Main Kit Computer Buy/Repair	0	0	0		0	0		0	0	0		0	0	
Main Kit. Maint.Conts.	407	1,477	-1,070	-72%	1,477	-1,070	-72%	3,192	5,654	-2,462	-44%	5,654	-2,462	-44%
Main Kit Kitchen Equipt.Reps	2,304	2,259	45	2%	2,259	45	2%	10,719	3,311	7,408	224%	3,311	7,408	224%
Main Kit. Hood Cleaning	0	473	-473		473	-473		1,818	3,144	-1,326	-42%	3,144	-1,326	-42%
Main Kit. Gen.Equipt.Reps	191	-26	217	-839%	-26	217	-839%	289	244	45	18%	244	45	18%
Main Kit. Refrig. Reps.	349	13	336	2,503%	13	336	2,503%	349	206	143	70%	206	143	70%
Main Kit Comp License/Suppor	0	0	0		0	0		0	0	0		0	0	
Main Kit. Floor/Carpet	90	0	90	0%	0	90	0%	540	0	540	0%	0	540	0%
Main Kit. Furniture	0	0	0		0	0		0	0	0		0	0	
Main Kit. Fittings	0	25	-25		25	-25		0	1,034	-1,034		1,034	-1,034	
Main Kit Small Equipment	187	0	187	0%	0	187	0%	1,128	0	1,128	0%	0	1,128	0%
Main Kit.Copier Rent/Chge	3	2	1	58%	2	1	58%	16	17	-1	-6%	17	-1	-6%
Main Kit.Copier Maint'nce	0	0	0		0	0		0	0	0		0	0	
Main Kit. Internet Costs	0	0	0		0	0		0	0	0		0	0	
Main Kit. E Mail Costs	0	0	0		0	0		0	0	0		0	0	
Main Kit. Other Mainten	0	0	0		0	0		0	0	0		0	0	
Main Kit. Maintenance Charges	0	266	-266		266	-266		0	1,067	-1,067		1,067	-1,067	
Main Kit Window Repairs	0	0	0		0	0		0	0	0		0	0	
Main Kit Health and Safety Equip	0	0	0		0	0		0	319	-319		319	-319	
Kit Operating Costs	**8,519**	**7,749**	770	**10%**	**7,766**	753	**10%**	**35,378**	**29,175**	6,203	**21%**	**29,047**	6,331	**22%**
As a % of Revenue	**4.81%**	**4.29%**			**4.52%**			**5.06%**	**4.45%**			**4.62%**		

	Actual	Budget	Var £	%	Last Year	Var £	%	Actual	Budget	Var £	%	Last Year	Var £	%
Payroll Costs	**£57,506**	**£63,657**	-£6,151	**-10%**	**£44,988**	£12,518	**28%**	**£222,249**	**£232,445**	-£10,196	**-4%**	**£173,967**	£48,282	**28%**
Operating Costs	**£8,519**	**£7,749**	£770	**10%**	**£7,766**	£753	**10%**	**£35,378**	**£29,175**	£6,203	**21%**	**£29,047**	£6,331	**22%**
Department Expense	**-£66,025**	**-£71,406**	£5,381	**-8%**	**-£52,754**	-£13,271	**25%**	**-£257,627**	**-£261,620**	£3,993	**-2%**	**-£203,014**	-£54,613	**27%**

COVERS	Actual	Budget	Var £	%	Last Year	Var £	%	Actual	Budget	Var £	%	Actual	Var £	%
Breakfast Covers	2,238	2,432	-194	-8%	2,356	-118	-5%	8,582	8,946	-364	-4%	8,491	91	1%
Rest Covers	1,980	1,900	80	4%	1,742	238	14%	7,200	7,350	-150	-2%	6,946	254	4%
R/Horse Checks	4,257	3,450	807	23%	3,355	902	27%	15,799	15,300	499	3%	14,997	802	5%
Functions + Events Cvrs	3,004	3,450	-446	-13%	3,412	-408	-12%	12,140	11,950	190	2%	11,906	234	2%
Cowdray Checks	3,511	3,450	61	2%	3,413	98	3%	13,869	14,050	-181	-1%	13,788	81	1%
TOTAL COVERS	**14,990**	**14,682**	308	**2%**	**14,278**	712	**5%**	**57,590**	**57,596**	-6	**0%**	**56,128**	1,462	**3%**

Figure 4.6 (Continued)

Our total revenues were £407,919 for the month and total costs were £66,025. This will then lead to important key measures such as departmental income or profit, Gross Operating Profit and potentially down to EBITDA level, depending on the measures used by the company. A kitchen is slightly unusual in terms of reporting, because as such a kitchen does not make revenue – usually any revenues are documented in the department "Food and Beverage", whereas from a P&L perspective a kitchen only has costs. However, we do keep track of the percentage of costs we need to make the revenue. In the example above, we used £8,519 in costs to make the £176,947 of food revenue – leading to a percentage of 4.81%. We do the same with payroll, to find out how much money we needed for all the labour as a percentage of the revenue we made. In the above, this is £57,506 for a revenue of £176,947 – a percentage of 32.5%.

In addition to showing the figures for the month just passed, the month end report shows a comparison of the figures vs. the budgeted amounts and vs. the results of the same month the year before. These comparisons are important to identify trends and understand the business performance over a period of time. Our total food revenue is £176,947 – £7,741 or 2% lower than the budget for the month which was £180,753. Compared to last year though, we made an increase of 3% or £5,044. When looking at the total year so far, we are in a good position – the actualized total food revenue of £699,511 is 7% or £43,798 higher than the budget of £655,713. Taken into account that parts of the Club have been under renovation throughout the year, this is a very healthy result. The figures also show that this time last year we had made £1.48 million in revenue, whereas this year we have already totalled £1.59 million – impressive 8% growth year on year.

Looking at payroll, even though we were £3,807 behind in revenue, we saved £6,151 in payroll costs. It is expected to make some savings when revenues are down, however we managed to work a lot more efficiently, as our payroll as a percentage of revenue totalled to 32.5% compared to a budget of 35.2% – a good achievement by the team. This was mainly as a result of saving of £6,603 in chef salaries, which were only replaced by £2,270 in agency chef costs. Because we paid less in fixed chef salaries, related expenses such as pension and tax contribution made by the Club also went down. For the year so far, we are showing good efficiency as the payroll percentage year to date is 31.7% vs. a budget of 35.4%. Looking at last year's figures, we have made a small drop in term of efficiency though, as last year we managed a percentage of 27.7%. We have worked hard to drive the quality of food in the Club up and it is natural that this means the percentage of payroll increases. It takes a lot more hours of chef labour to prepare a fresh lobster dish than it does to make a burger and chips. The strategy of a kitchen (i.e. the type of food it wants to prepare) should be reflected in its budget. It is impossible to deliver high quality food and gourmet dinners if there is no money in the budget to pay the chefs needed to make this happen.

Though it is great to show a decrease in payroll vs. revenue, there are some dangers attached to it long term if it is a continuing trend. If people are pushed to work harder or longer, this can show great results financially. However, this may have an impact on their motivation, job satisfaction and energy levels. If work is being done by too small a group of people for a continuous period, this may lead to people leaving and increased turnover – efficiency is good, but putting unnecessary pressure on people may have an adverse effect in the long term.

Our expenses (the costs of the equipment needed to run the kitchen) were £770 higher than budget and £753 higher than last year. As our food revenue was below budget, ideally our expenses should have been as well. In terms of percentage, it shows that with 4.81% we used slightly more equipment than budgeted, as the budget was 4.29%. The actual costs of expenses and payroll make it clear how significant the payroll costs are. All the equipment needed cost a total of £8,519, but the payroll needed was £57,506 – showing that keeping payroll cost in control is very important. The section in grey shows that even though operating costs were 10% higher than budget, the total costs for the department were 8% lower than budget. This is because the 10% saving in payroll costs is such a large amount of money saved. Compared to last year, our expenses were £13k higher. This may seem bad; however, we should not forget we also made £5k more in revenue than last year so it is natural that more money was spent.

The last section shows the analysis of covers. It shows that we did not welcome as many guests for breakfast as budgeted (2,238 vs. 2,432), however that the Dining Room, the Running Horse pub and the Cowdray lounge did more covers than budgeted. Functions and events were down, with 13% less covers than budgeted. Year to date however, functions and events has done 190 covers more than budgeted whereas the dining room has done 150 less than budgeted – a different picture than when looking at the month of April alone. Keep in mind that these figures only display covers and do not specify average check. Even though the dining room has welcomed 150 guests less than budgeted, if every guest that we did welcome spent more money than budgeted, then in the end the result may still be very positive. The same situation can happen with room occupancy: if fewer rooms are sold however, each room is sold for a higher price than budgeted, the total room revenue may still be higher than budget even though occupancy is down.

When comparing figures to budget, it is important to note that the budget that the monthly figures are being compared to is usually drafted around September the year before. Many different circumstances can change between September the year before and the actual month itself taking place. For example, nobody would have known in September 2016 that London would suffer two terrorist attacks in March and June 2017. Major incidents like these can have a big impact on visitor numbers coming in to a city or area and it is important to keep recent developments in mind when discussing figures compared to a budget drafted many months ago. Another, more innocent cause of variances year on year may be as simple as the fact that Easter falls in one month one year and another the next year. Some businesses re-forecast their revenues and expenses of the upcoming months on a monthly basis and therefore do not work with a comparison to budget in month end reports but instead compare the monthly results to the most recent forecast.

Regardless of which comparison is used, it is up to the managers to critically look at the numbers and think about where potential variances may come from. For example, a business that is only in its second year of operation may show extraordinary increases compared to last year, whereas a business that is undergoing renovation and therefore does not have full use of all its rooms or outlets may show significant drops compared to last year. When analysing this, it may turn out that a drop year on year is still a good result when taking in to account the reduced availability of facilities.

Forecast

Most of the descriptions above are related to measurements and figures that describe or reflect performance in the past. There is another set of figures that is used which focuses on the future and these numbers are referred to as the forecast. Some businesses have formal forecasting cycles where managers and the finance team publish their best forecast of the upcoming three months on a monthly basis. Other businesses have a less formal approach to it and discuss their general estimation of where the business is going to go in a weekly meeting. For some areas in hospitality, the Revenue Management team may even publish a revised forecast of room revenues every working day based on their continuous analysis and comparisons to the competitive set. Our Club does not have the same systems in place as a global hotel or restaurant chain may do, so in our case forecasting is done in a rather informal way by looking at the business on the books and discussing our expectations for what other business may still come up in the future.

Forecasting is an important practice as it gives managers an indication of what is ahead and gives them an opportunity to plan costs in accordance with the forecast. All three main cost areas within the kitchen should be reviewed if there is a change in the forecasted numbers. Food cost is a result of daily purchases and therefore should be quite flexible in nature. However, there may be *standing orders* (fixed orders that are repeated every day or week) for items that we need every day in roughly the same amounts, such as breakfast pastries, bread rolls, yoghurt, fresh whole fruits or orange juice. If the forecast shows a significant increase or decrease in expected business, these orders need to be adjusted as otherwise we would end up with either too little or too much stock.

In terms of payroll, the first changes to make if a forecast is showing less business than usual would be to lower the amount of agency shifts and solely work with the full-time chefs. If the situation is more serious and cutting agency spend will not be sufficient to hit the payroll percentage target, other options would be to allow more people to go on holiday. Though this is an option that Finance often references to when numbers are not looking too good, it is a hard measure to put in place without damaging staff morale, as nobody likes to be sent on holiday during a time of year where they did not request holidays. Another option would be to *hold a vacancy*, meaning for the moment not actively recruiting for a vacant position or postponing the start date of a position.

For equipment costs, items such as cling film, piping bags etc. will automatically decrease as less business requires less of them to be used. One may be inclined to postpone the purchasing of small kitchen equipment such as a new blender or waterbath when business is low. However, in most businesses any money that was budgeted for equipment in a month which is not spent in that same month is lost. Therefore, it is advisable to discuss these things with the Finance team and explain that even though a purchase can be postponed to a month where revenues are higher, the purchase still needs to be made.

In contrast, when the forecast is looking very healthy, i.e. with lots of revenue planned to come in, it is important for a manager to address any costs that need to be added to deal with the increase in incoming business. If the Club would continuously be significantly above budget in terms of guests and the forecast shows this is expected to continue, it is up to us to build a business case to explain an additional chef is needed to help us serve these guests in line with our high standards. Similarly, if we see that our breakfast *capture ratio* (the percentage of guests that have breakfast in the Club) has been significantly higher than expected for a considerable length of time, additional buffet equipment such as display baskets, toasters or juice dispensers may need to be purchased even though they were not originally budgeted.

Conclusion

Managing the financial health of a kitchen is down to combining all relevant information available and making sound decisions based on what various reports show. Relationships with suppliers, events and restaurant teams and the finance team are essential to avoid unpleasant surprises and keep a grip on the costs of running a kitchen. Food cost and payroll are the two main influencers of the financial state of a kitchen so if nothing else, these need to be monitored closely and adjusted depending on historical results and future forecasts. There is a lot of money involved in the operation of a professional kitchen. Even though many Chefs starting out in the industry are mainly focused on preparing beautiful meals for guests, as careers progress managing costs and teams becomes increasingly important. As all managers, Chefs have a duty to take care of their guests, their teams, and their profits – the key is to balance all these various factors successfully.

Second edition "epilogue"

Five years on from COVID-19 and in many ways, we're still measuring the true impact on hospitality. In some ways it has been a resetting of the scales, with a long historic disproportionate cost expectation from guests to businesses to suppliers.

One of the most significant changes was its influence on staffing, as many experienced chefs left the industry, some due to relocation back to their native country, others due to concerns about work-life balance, or the financial instability caused by lockdowns. The resulting staff shortages made recruitment a major challenge. This led to a bidding war and "over-promotions", resulting in the Royal Airforce Club expanding its partnerships with universities and offering more apprenticeships – a newly introduced national insurance saving on apprenticeships helping employers offset costs of higher salaries.

The skill level that used to be the norm for each level of chef had to be adjusted down to fill vacancies and menus simplified to maintain consistency. The disruption to supply chains led to significant challenges in the availability of produce, which in turn drove up prices. Businesses faced delays, inconsistent deliveries, and shortages of key ingredients, which forced chefs to adapt menus and become more resourceful with what was available. Many high-end restaurants decided to forgo the a la carte offering and stick to the more cost-controlled tasting menu. The price of ingredients soared due to inflationary pressures.

All of these changes made it harder to maintain profitability and inevitably this led to many businesses closing. It also urged chefs to be more creative and innovative in their selection of ingredients. As an example, we started using cuts of meat and fish that would have not featured on menus as much pre-Covid.

The pandemic was arguably the biggest challenge of recent years, but it has accelerated the industry's need to re-think working practices, spurred it on to find new efficiencies and reinforced its resilience. After the dust settled, we returned to the "new normal" which fundamentally meant working towards the same percentages and targets previously demanded of us. Thankfully, we also learned people's urge to travel and explore new and old destinations did not dissipate. The rollercoaster of Covid proved that hospitality remains an invaluable sector of any developed economy and a fantastic career choice.

Notes

1 Non-linear costs, a fourth type of cost behaviour, is beyond the scope of our discussion. Interested readers should review a good managerial accounting textbook (e.g. Horngren, Foster and Datar, 2006).

2 *Marginal cost* is often used interchangeably with incremental cost. But they are not always the same as marginal cost is the derivative of the cost function. A derivative is a concept from calculus that involves the *instantaneous rate of change* of a variable with respect to some other variable. While a discussion of calculus and derivatives is beyond the scope of this chapter, we state without proof that marginal cost is incremental cost (which is also variable cost) for a mixed cost.

3 In other settings (e.g. manufacturing firms) the procedures are complex and multiple approaches to cost estimation are used. Explanation of these methods is beyond the scope of this chapter and interested readers should review a good managerial accounting textbook (e.g. Horngren, Foster and Datar, 2006).

4 The assumption is that this change in sales volume is within the relevant range and the cost estimates remain unchanged. If management believes the actual output volume would have resulted in a different cost structure (i.e. different total fixed cost and unit variable cost), the flex budget would use the different cost equation at the actual sales volume of 110,000 hamburgers.

CHAPTER

5 Capital budgeting

Planning for long-term asset expenditure

Learning outcomes

At the end of this chapter, readers should:

- understand the importance of ongoing capital investment in hospitality firms;
- differentiate between the accounting treatment of capital investment and repair and maintenance expenditure;
- understand the notion of the time value of money;
- be able to apply investment appraisal techniques.

THEORY

James W. Hesford and Michael J. Turner

Introduction

The purpose of this chapter is to give you the knowledge and tools to evaluate long-term capital investments. In addition to day-to-day operational decision-making, hospitality managers also engage in planning. They develop short- and long-term budgets, and frequently make decisions and/or recommendations for long-term capital investments. Capital budgeting is the term used to describe the process of developing budgets for capital investment. Long-term capital investments establish a firm's capabilities and frequently define the identity of a firm. The firm's survival depends on the firm making the right decisions. Capital investments require large cash outlays and have a long-term impact on future profitability. Undertaking a "bad" project could lead to bankruptcy, whereas not undertaking a "good" project could make the firm less competitive, also threatening its long-term viability. Accordingly, hospitality managers must effectively plan for long-term capital investment.

DOI: 10.4324/9781003545903-5

In every hospitality organisation there is an ongoing need to replace assets, assets that include furniture, fixtures and equipment (FF&E). Further, hospitality firms operate in highly uncertain and competitive environments, with demand fluctuating due to the economy, terrorist events, natural disasters and customers' preferences. Competing in this environment, managers must think strategically about capital investment. For example, given a limited amount of funding, should the hotel expand by acquiring additional assets (e.g. a swimming pool or fitness facility) or should some existing assets be upgraded?

To appreciate the importance of capital investment appraisal skills, consider that average annual capital investment (also known as capital expenditure, or CapEx) spending for full-service hotels is 9% of total revenue (ISHC, 2023). In other words, full-service hotels appreciate that ongoing CapEx for the building, equipment, rooms, lobby, ballroom, meeting spaces, food and beverage outlets, etc. are necessary to sustain competitive advantage.

Related to capital investment is the considerable repair and maintenance (R&M) expenditure necessary to retain the hotel's investment value. Capital investment and R&M are closely related. Excessive R&M expenditure may hint at deferred capital investment, or an obsolete building and its equipment. Small R&M expenditure may be due to new assets, or hint at future excessive R&M expenditures. For example, a manager who defers repairing a leaking roof will have higher repair costs when water damages the roof structure, guest room walls and ceilings, and so forth. Annual R&M expenditure is about half that of capital investment, at 4.4% of total revenue (ISHC, 2023).

In the next section we illustrate capital investment and its importance, including how one distinguishes between CapEx and R&M expenditure. We then explain the financial models used to evaluate capital investment. These models, or analytical tools, include: net present value, internal rate of return, modified internal rate of return, payback, modified payback, accounting rate of return, and profitability index. At the conclusion of the chapter we provide a discussion and recap key points.

Capital investment and its importance

According to most accounting standards, capital investments are considered to occur when money is spent for assets whose returns are expected to continue beyond the current year. More specifically, capital investment is a cash flow to acquire land, structures (i.e., buildings) and equipment with a useful life of more than a single year.

Despite a seemingly-clear definition, a key issue that hospitality managers face is whether to treat expenditures as capital investment or as R&M. There is frequent confusion on the distinction, and you should be aware that there can be significant subjectivity in the accounting treatment for these types of expenditures. For example, consider a hotel replacing all of its bellhop luggage trolleys. It is probably capital investment, but if they keep the wheels and replace everything else, could we now classify total expense as R&M expenditure? Are we repairing the trolleys because we're not buying new ones? The point we are trying to make is that, in some situations, there is no black-and-white decision rule. This can be problematic since the decision will have an impact on amounts reported in the firm's financial statements. Expenditures treated as capital investment are capitalised, meaning that we record an asset on the balance sheet. This results in future depreciation expense over the useful life of the asset. Income in the current period is increased relative to treating the expenditure as R&M, and future periods will have lower income. However, expenditures treated as R&M are expensed in the period incurred, resulting in much lower income relative to what would be obtained if the expenditure were capitalised. Future income will be higher as there is no future depreciation expense associated with the R&M expenditure.

To further illustrate the impact of capital investment versus R&M expenditure, consider the following scenario: $20,000 is spent to replace most of the parts on the hotel's bell-hop luggage trolleys (classify the trolleys as part of "equipment"). Assume there is subjectivity in the manager's decision to capitalise or expense the expenditure. Further assume that, if capitalised, the trolleys would be estimated to have a useful life of four years with zero salvage value (i.e. no value for the asset at the end of its life). Panel A of Table 5.1 summarises how this capital investment impacts the balance sheet and income statement if straight-line depreciation method were used for the trolleys. Panel B shows the alternative scenario of treating the expenditure as R&M.

The impact of treating the expenditure as capital investment results, in Year 1, in an asset being recognised on the balance sheet at a book value of $20,000 (see Table 5.1, panel A). There is no impact on the income statement as the transaction exchanges two assets: cash for equipment. In each of the four years, there is a $5,000 reduction in the net book value of the equipment due to the depreciation expense ($20,000 / 4 years for straight-line depreciation), the amount being added each year to the balance sheet as accumulated depreciation. The annual depreciation is an expense on the income statement of $5,000, reducing the hotel's annual profits to $7,500.

However, if the $20,000 expense were treated as R&M, the entire amount is expensed in Year 1 (see Panel B of Table 5.1). With this large expense, the hotel will report a loss of $7,500. The impact to the balance sheet is immediate: There is a $7,500 decrease in retained earnings in Year 1. However, over the next three years, there is no depreciation expense (since no asset was

Table 5.1 The impact of capital investment vs. repair and maintenance expenditure

Panel A: Treatment as capital investment				
Balance sheet				
	Year 1	*Year 2*	*Year 3*	*Year 4*
Investment (i.e. book value)	$20,000	$20,000	$20,000	$20,000
Less: Accumulated depreciation	($5,000)	($10,000)	($15,000)	($20,000)
Net book value	$15,000	$10,000	$5,000	$0
Income statement				
Revenue	$12,500	$12,500	$12,500	$12,500
Less: Depreciation expense	($5,000)	($5,000)	($5,000)	($5,000)
Repair and maintenance expense	–	–	–	–
Profit (loss)	$7,500	$7,500	$7,500	$7,500

Panel B: Treatment as repair and maintenance expenditure				
Balance Sheet				
	Year 1	*Year 2*	*Year 3*	*Year 4*
Investment (i.e. book value)	–	–	–	–
Less: Accumulated depreciation	–	–	–	–
Net book value	–	–	–	–
Income statement				
	Year 1	*Year 2*	*Year 3*	*Year 4*
Revenue	$12,500	$12,500	$12,500	$12,500
Less: Depreciation expense	–	–	–	–
Repair and maintenance expense	($20,000)	($0)	($0)	($0)
Profit (loss)	($7,500)	$12,500	$12,500	$12,500

created) and annual profit is $12,500. Note the total profit over the four periods is the same for both treatments; differences are simply a matter of timing.

The takeaway from this illustration is the fact that the choice between whether to capitalise or expense an expenditure will have an impact on the published financial statements. And this may further impact the hotel's ability to raise capital and meet performance benchmarks. The impact will likely extend to the manager, as her compensation is most likely contingent upon achieving specific, annual performance benchmarks.[1]

Investment appraisal

Time value of money

Introduction

Imagine you loaned a friend \$100 yesterday and he promised to pay you back today. However, today your friend says that he is having financial problems and wants to pay the loan back one year from now. Would you prefer \$100 today or \$100 one year from now? From experience, you know that the price of goods is usually going up each year. That is, the cost of a \$25,000 automobile might be \$27,500 one year from now. Or an article of clothing that costs \$50 today will likely cost \$55 next year. While not all commodities increase at the same rate (as the 10% example used here), there is some average increase in prices over time. Therefore, if your friend pays you back one year from now, you would not be able to buy as much "stuff" when the loan is repaid next year. The point here is that there is a "time value" to money. The sum of monies received over time (i.e. future cash flows) is not equal in value to the same amount today.

You explain this to your friend and he offers to pay back more than \$100 so that you would not suffer a financial setback from helping him out. But how much should your friend pay? There are two factors to consider when thinking about how much your friend should repay you. First, there is the rise in prices one year from now, and this increase is referred to as *inflation*. The second factor concerns compensating you for the possibility that you may never be repaid. That is, you agree to wait for the loan to be repaid but, over the course of the year, your friend could die, could have a falling out with you (and refuse to pay you back), or the two of you may simply forget about the loan. The possibility of *default* can be compensated for, or priced. Considering both factors, you and your friend agree on a future amount to be repaid. Suppose the two of you decide that he will pay back \$115. In this case, we say that the \$100 is the repayment of the principal amount of the loan, and the \$15 is the *interest* on the loan that compensates you for the two factors (again, these being inflation risk and default risk). Interest is normally expressed as a rate in *percentage* terms as the repayment above the amount borrowed, relative to the amount borrowed. Using the example here, the interest rate is calculated as ((\$115 – \$100) / \$100) × 100 = (\$15 / \$100) × 100 = 15%.

Another way of thinking about this is that, if your friend repaid the loan today, you could make an investment in an asset (e.g. a bank deposit) that will provide you with the right to receive \$115 a year from now. When your friend doesn't pay back his loan today, you have an *opportunity cost* (i.e. income foregone since the investment opportunity is lost) that must be compensated for by your friend. When considering the opportunity cost, one must ensure that the overall risk of the alternative investment (in this example, the bank deposit) is the same level of risk as the loan to your friend!

Determining the present value of future cash flows

First, let the amount of money invested today be represented by the variable, *PV*. Next, let future value (i.e. the amount received at the end of the period) be represented by *FV*. Finally, let the interest rate be represented by *i*. Drawing on the example illustrated above, the future value of an investment today can be represented as follows:

$$FV_1 = PV + i \times PV = PV \times (1+i) \qquad 5.1$$

where the subscript "1" refers to the cash flow occurring at the end of period 1. What is the future value if our investment is kept for two periods?

$$FV_2 = FV_1 + i \times FV_1 = FV_1 \times (1+i) \qquad 5.2$$

In other words, the future value at the end of period 2 (as indicated by the subscript "2") is equal to the future value at period 1 plus the interest earned on that amount during the second period. Now replace FV_1 in Equation 5.2 with the right-hand-side of Equation 5.1 to obtain:

$$FV_2 = FV_1 \times (1+i) = PV \times (1+i) \times (1+i) = PV \times (1+i)^2 \qquad 5.3$$

Extending this to the third period, one will find that $FV_3 = PV \times (1 + i)^3$. And so on, where the future value for any period, *n*, is given by $FV_n = PV \times (1 + i)^n$. The expression $(1 + i)^n$ is called the *future value interest factor*, the amount by which the present value is multiplied to result in some future value. If the interest earned remains invested with the principal, we refer to this process as "*compounding*". The future value formula assumes compounding. Figure 5.1 shows the growth in future value over multiple time periods using our $100 loan example.

Using algebra, we can re-write the future value formula to solve for present value, *PV*. We have:

$$PV = FV_n / (1+i)^n \qquad 5.4$$

The factor operating on FV_n, $1 / (1 + i)^n$, is called the *present value interest factor*. It is the amount by which the future value is reduced to yield its present value, *PV*. Since this formula is the "reverse process" from the future value formula, the term "*discounting*" refers to finding the present value of some future amount and $(1 + i)^n$ is also known as the discount factor. To determine the present value of a future cash flow, it is necessary to *discount* a future cash flow by the amount its value has diminished.

Two things are worth remembering: (1) For a given interest rate, the greater the number of periods, the lower the present value; and, (2) for

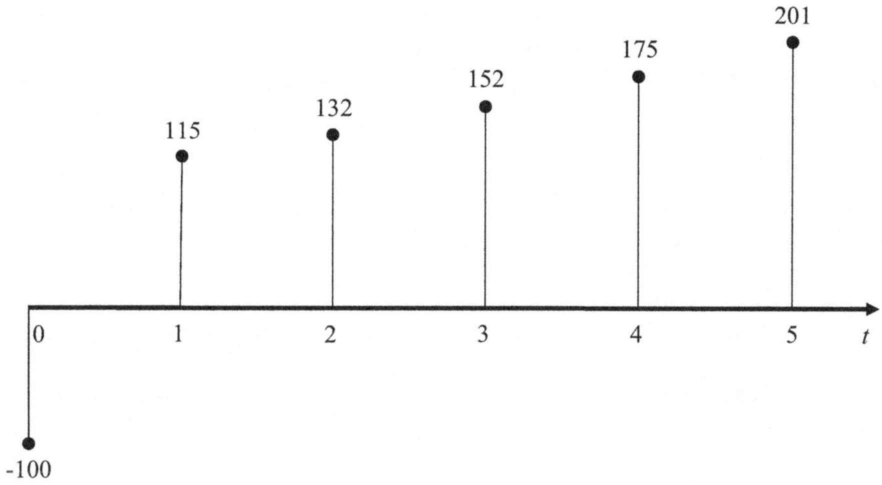

Figure 5.1 Growth in future value over time

a given time period, the higher the interest rate, the lower the present value.

The present value and future value calculations are straightforward when using calculators with math functions (in particular, a key labelled x^y). Financial calculators (such as the HP 12C or TI BA II Plus) and spreadsheets (e.g. Excel or Numbers) make the task simpler yet through dedicated functions.

Assumptions

In developing the formulas above, we want to make explicit several assumptions, these being:

1. The investment (initial cash flow) occurs at the beginning of the period (i.e. time zero, $t = 0$).
2. Subsequent cash flows (in and out) occur at the end of a period. Since most capital budgeting projects are long term, this means that cash flows occur at the end of the year. While unrealistic, this usually does not cause problems as the cash flow amounts are forecasts (often with significant errors) and the timeframes are long. If this assumption is problematic, periods can be reduced to months, weeks or days. However, with short-term periods, there are errors in forecasting the timing of cash flows.

3. The firm will reinvest future cash inflows at a return equal to its required rate of return (i.e. its cost of capital).
4. The interest rate, *i*, is constant across all periods.

Techniques

This section describes common investment appraisal techniques. As capital budgeting involves decisions where cash flows extend beyond the current year, it is necessary to consider the time value of money. We refer to this as *discounted cash-flow* (DCF) *analysis*, and there are two popular methods: Net Present Value (NPV) and Internal Rate of Return (IRR). After presenting the popular DCF techniques, we present five alternatives, two of which are non-DCF methods: Modified IRR, Payback, Modified payback, Accounting rate of return, and Profitability index.

Net present value

NPV is the sum of the present values of all cash flows related to an investment. The first step is to estimate the firm's interest rate, *i*, that appears in the present value formula derived above. The interest rate used in the PV calculations is the firm's *required rate of return, r*. The interest rate is sometimes referred to as *minimum desired rate of return, cost of capital* or *discount rate*. When computing NPV it is possible to select different interest rates for different time periods, although practitioners frequently assume interest rates are the same for all periods as this makes analysis simpler. The interest rate varies for each firm, based on their cost of raising capital, and may also vary across time. The decision rule is to accept any project that has an NPV greater than zero.

> *Example.* To illustrate NPV calculations, consider the case of an economy-lodging firm with an investment opportunity at one of its hotel properties. A vacant building adjacent to its property was once the site of a popular, family-style restaurant. Senior executives of the firm have been considering whether to purchase the building and lot to develop and operate its own restaurant.
>
> After doing market research and hiring a restaurant consultant, the firm gathered the information needed to decide whether to develop the restaurant. Purchasing the former restaurant and improving the building would require a $750,000 investment for furniture, kitchen equipment, flooring and other construction. The firm expects to obtain cash flows of $250,000 in each of the following five years. At the end of Year 5, the firm expects to sell the restaurant. Further, senior executives of the firm believe market demographics are evolving, and they predict the building and associated land will net $850,000 at the end of the fifth year.

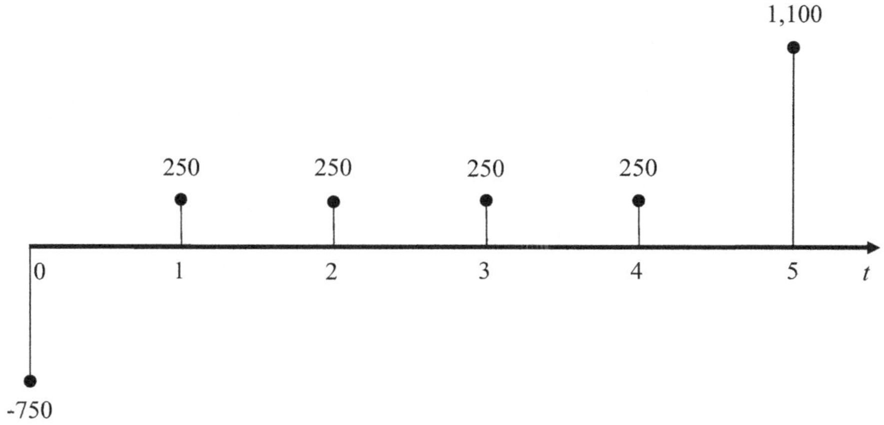

Figure 5.2 Timeline of cash flows

The timeline in Figure 5.2 depicts these cash flows. Vertical line segments drawn below the horizontal axis (which represents time, t, in years) represent cash outflows (i.e. negative cash flows from investments or period losses) while vertical line segments above the horizontal axis represent cash inflows (i.e. period profits and asset sales).

The firm has determined that its required rate of return, r, is 10%. When practitioners refer to the "required rate of return", they commonly use the variable r in place of i in the formulas; this is a simple "cosmetic" change. Making this substitution, recall the formula for the present value (PV) of a future cash flow: $PV_n = CF_n / (1 + r)^n$. Also recall that the index n refers to a specific cash flow in the nth period (years, as described in the timeline discussion above). The general formula for NPV can be compactly expressed as $\text{NPV} = \sum_{i=0}^{n} CF_i / (1+r)^i$, where the Greek letter sigma (Σ) represents the sum over a range of values (in this case, from 0 to some value, n). We now calculate the present value (rounded) of the firm's five future cash flows.

$$PV_1 = \$250{,}000 / (1 + 0.10)^1 = \$250{,}000 / 1.10 = \$227{,}273$$
$$PV_2 = \$250{,}000 / (1 + 0.10)^2 = \$250{,}000 / 1.21 = \$206{,}612$$
$$PV_3 = \$250{,}000 / (1 + 0.10)^3 = \$250{,}000 / 1.33 = \$187{,}829$$
$$PV_4 = \$250{,}000 / (1 + 0.10)^4 = \$250{,}000 / 1.46 = \$170{,}753$$
$$PV_5 = \$1{,}100{,}000 / (1 + 0.10)^5 = \$1{,}100{,}000 / 1.61 = \$683{,}013$$

The sum of the five present values is $1,475,480. From this, subtract the initial investment of $750,000 to obtain an NPV of $725,480. Since NPV is greater than zero, the firm will create wealth for its owners if it opens with the new restaurant.

Internal rate of return

IRR is conceptually similar, but with IRR one asks: "What interest rate would generate an NPV = 0?" An alternative way to express this is that the IRR is the interest rate that would make the present value of future cash flows equal to the investment (i.e. the initial cash flow). NPV is set to zero because this is the point at which the investment is between destroying value (i.e. NPV < 0) and creating value (i.e. NPV > 0) for the firm. Setting the NPV formula equal to zero, we have:

$$CF_1 / (1 + i)^1 + CF_2 / (1 + i)^2 + \ldots + CF_n / (1 + i)^n + CF_0 = 0$$

Similar to the NPV formula, we can write this compactly as $\sum_{j=0}^{n} CF_j / (1+i)^j = 0$. Note that for any value of i, the denominator will be one for the initial investment (which occurs at time zero) because any number raised to the zeroth power is 1; in other words, the current period cash flow (negative, since it's the investment being made) is not discounted as it is a present, not future, cash flow.

Unlike NPV, where one has estimated the interest rate and calculates a present value, with IRR one must find the value of i that makes the sum of the cash flows equal to zero. Unfortunately, there is no closed-form equation that can be used to solve for i. If done by hand, the solution is found iteratively and can take a while. In other words, a value of i must be tried, then a second value of i is tried, a third and so on until the present value of all cash flows sum to zero. As with NPV calculations, a financial calculator or spreadsheet provides a fast calculation for IRR.

The decision rule is to accept a project if its IRR is greater than the firm's "hurdle rate". Since the required rate of return isn't computed for IRR, hurdle rate refers to the minimum interest rate needed for management to undertake a project. This phrase is analogous to a hurdle race, a track event in which barriers must be leaped by runners (or horses) competing in the event. In other words, the project must "clear" an interest rate hurdle in order to be considered for funding.

At this point you may be wondering: "if IRR is more difficult to calculate, why not just calculate NPV?" The answer is that there is one benefit to using IRR: it is not necessary for the analyst to compute the firm's required rate of return. The required rate of return is the firm's cost of capital and estimating this number is no simple feat.[2] Accordingly, senior managers typically set a hurdle rate well above what they believe is the firm's cost of capital. What this means is that the firm may sometimes reject projects that are worthwhile (i.e. that would create value for the firm).

A difficulty with using IRR exists when a firm has an existing asset that could be (1) sold today or (2) developed further to receive future cash flows. IRR for the development project can be computed, but it is not possible to compute IRR for the alternative of selling the current asset. In other words, one cannot compare a percentage return (IRR for the development project) with a dollar amount (proceeds from selling the existing asset). With NPV, no problem exists: The decision involves comparing the NPV of the development to the cash inflow from selling the existing asset.

> *Example.* To illustrate the IRR calculation, consider the project discussed above. Assume that management has set a hurdle rate of 15% for new projects. Recall that, at a required rate of return (i.e. interest rate) of 10%, the project's NPV is \$725,480. A higher interest rate will reduce the present value of future cash flows, so IRR must be greater than 10%. (Recall we noted that, for a given time period, a higher interest rate results in a lower present value.) Also recall that there is no simple solution to finding the required return, r. Trying $r = 25\%$, NPV is computed as follows:

$$NPV = \$250{,}000 / (1 + 0.25)^1 + \$250{,}000 / (1 + 0.25)^2 + \$250{,}000 / (1 + 0.25)^3 + \$250{,}000 / (1 + 0.25)^4 + \$1{,}100{,}000 / (1 + 0.25)^5 - \$750{,}000 = \$200{,}848$$

Since NPV > 0, IRR must be greater than 25%. NPV dropped significantly so try a smaller increment in r, perhaps using $r = 35\%$. NPV is:

$$NPV = \$250{,}000 / (1 + 0.35)^1 + \$250{,}000 / (1 + 0.35)^2 + \$250{,}000 / (1 + 0.35)^3 + \$250{,}000 / (1 + 0.35)^4 + \$1{,}100{,}000 / (1 + 0.35)^5 - \$750{,}000 = -\$5{,}448$$

Since NPV < 0, IRR is less than 35%. Trying different values of r, NPV is 0 when r is approximately 34.7%. Therefore, IRR for the project is 34.7%. Since IRR is greater than the firm's required rate of return, the project should be accepted. By plotting NPV for a range of rates of return (r), the relationship between these two variables can be visualized. From this plot, IRR is found to be a bit below 35% (i.e. the point where the curve intercepts the x-axis, which is at NPV = 0). See Figure 5.3.

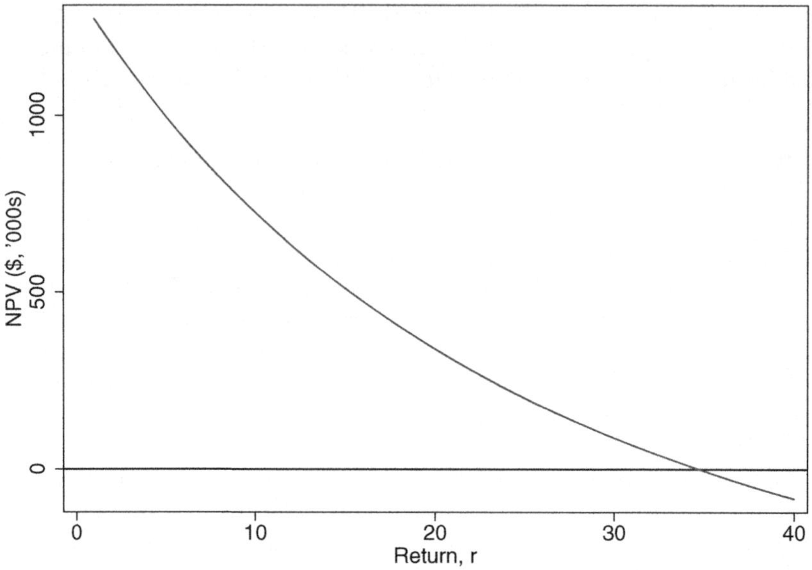

Figure 5.3 The relationship between net present value and the required rate of return

Modified IRR

An assumption of discounted cash flow techniques is that future cash flows are re-invested at the calculated internal rate of return. This assumption is not always true.

When false, modified IRR solves this problem by allowing the analyst to select the re-investment interest rate. The analyst begins by taking the project cash flows to the *end* of the project, summing these to create a "terminal value". Next, the analyst finds the interest rate that equates the investment cost with the terminal value for the estimated life of the project.

> *Example.* Using the project from above, the future values (i.e. at $t = 5$ and a reinvestment rate of 10%) are as follows:

$$FV_{CF1} = \$250{,}000 \times (1 + 0.10)^4 = \$250{,}000 \times 1.46 = \$366{,}025$$
$$FV_{CF2} = \$250{,}000 \times (1 + 0.10)^3 = \$250{,}000 \times 1.33 = \$332{,}750$$
$$FV_{CF3} = \$250{,}000 \times (1 + 0.10)^2 = \$250{,}000 \times 1.21 = \$302{,}500$$
$$FV_{CF4} = \$250{,}000 \times (1 + 0.10)^1 = \$250{,}000 \times 1.10 = \$275{,}000$$
$$FV_{CF5} = \qquad = \$1{,}100{,}000$$

The sum of these future values – the *terminal value* – is \$2,376,275. This terminal value is just FV when we apply the formula $FV_n = PV \times (1 + i)^n$. Applying this formula to our example, we have: $\$2{,}376{,}275 = \$750{,}000 \times$

$(1 + i)^5$. Solve for i by dividing both sides by \$750,000 and take the fifth root of both sides: $(\$2{,}376{,}275 / \$750{,}000)^{1/5} = 1 + i = 3.17^{0.20} = 1.2594$. Therefore, $i = 1.2594 - 1 = 0.2594$, or 25.94%. Excel has a function to compute MIRR.

Payback

Payback period is one of the two non-DCF techniques used by practitioners. Payback period is the amount of time for the after-tax cash inflows from a project to sum to the amount of the original investment. That is, each period (typically, one year) a proportion of the capital investment is "paid back" to the firm that contributed the capital for the project investment. Each period's cash flows are deducted from the initial cost until the invested total is "recovered". The decision rule is to accept projects whose payback period is below some established criterion. The key limitation of this technique is that it ignores cash flows beyond the payback period. Another important limitation is that there is no adjustment for the time value of money (i.e. for inflation and risk); there is simply no way to know whether a project creates value for the firm. Nevertheless, it remains a fairly-popular rule because of the simplicity of the calculation. This is, however, not a good reason for its use. Anecdotal evidence suggests that payback periods are usually a relatively short time period (e.g. three years or five years). Like with IRR, the payback decision rule tends to be overly conservative and firms run the risk of rejecting projects that would ultimately create value for the firm.

> *Example.* Consider again the project used in the NPV and IRR examples. To simplify the problem (with no loss in generality), assume there are no taxes. During the course of Year 1, cash inflows were \$250,000. Having recovered \$250,000, the amount left to be "paid back" is \$750,000 − \$250,000 = \$500,000. At the end of Year 2 another \$250,000 is paid back. The remaining balance to be paid back is now \$250,000, and that amount is returned by the end of Year 3. Therefore, the payback period is three years. In most problems there is a balance at the end of a particular period and an excess is paid back during the course of the next period. In these cases, the payback period is not an integer (e.g. 3.7 years).[3] If the company's decision rule was a payback of 3.5 years, management would undertake this project since paying back the investment occurs in three years, before the criterion of 3.5 years.

Modified payback

The modified payback technique replaces the actual cash flows with *discounted* cash flows, similar to NPV. The modified payback period is the amount of time for the discounted, after-tax cash inflows from a project to sum to the amount of the original investment. As with the payback technique, modified payback ignores cash flows beyond the payback period. This remains as an important limitation of the modified payback technique. Like the Payback method, the decision rule is to accept projects whose payback period is less than some established criterion.

Example. Continuing with this chapter's example problem, the first three discounted future cash flows sum to $621,713. Whereas the payback method had a payback period of 3 years, the discounted method will need one or more additional periods since our initial cash outlay (i.e. investment) was $750,000. The "balance" to be paid back is $128,287, an amount that is paid back during Year 4 since the discounted cash flow that period is $170,753. Since "too much" has been paid back by the end of Year 4, it is common to calculate partial years as the "unpaid balance" divided by the cash flow in the "last" year. In this example the remaining balance is paid back in $128,287 / $170,753 = 0.75 years. Note that this calculation assumes daily cash flows, a departure from what was assumed with NPV and IRR calculations (although the discounting was done annually, not daily). The payback period is 3.75 years. If, as mentioned above, the company's decision rule was a payback of 3.5 years, management would reject this project since the payback period (3.75 years) exceeds the criterion of 3.5 years.

ACCOUNTING RATE OF RETURN

Accounting rate of return (ARR) is the average annual income for a project divided by the average annual investment. Accounting income is computed by subtracting the project's annual depreciation expense from the annual cash flow, then computing the average value over all years. The depreciation method and salvage value obviously impacts the ARR calculation. There are important limitations associated with this appraisal technique: First, the time value of money is ignored (i.e. it is a non-DCF appraisal technique); and, second, the method uses accounting income and book values rather than cash flows and market values. The decision rule is to accept projects whose ARR is above some established criterion.

Example. The table below was created using data from our example project. Recall that the final year cash flow includes cash from the sale of the hotel (i.e. the asset's salvage value). Assume the project will be depreciated using the straight-line method and that the firm's ARR criterion is 25%. With a $750,000 investment and a 5-year asset life, annual depreciation expense is $750,000 / 5 = $150,000. We obtain:

Table 5.2 Calculating accounting rate of return for our example project

Year	*Cash flow ($)*	*Accounting income ($)*	*Ending book value ($)*	*Average book value ($)*
1	250,000	100,000	600,000	675,000
2	250,000	100,000	450,000	525,000
3	250,000	100,000	300,000	375,000
4	250,000	100,000	150,000	225,000
5	1,100,000	950,000	0	75,000
Average	270,000			375,000

The ARR for the project is $270,000 / $375,000 = 0.72, or 72%. Since this ARR is above the firm's 25% criterion, the project would be accepted.

Profitability index

Profitability index (PI) is the final assessment technique we discuss in this chapter. PI measures the benefit per unit cost of a project, incorporating the time value of money. PI is calculated as the present value of inflows divided by the present value of outflows. PI is similar to NPV and fairly easy for individuals to comprehend. This measure is helpful if there are multiple competing projects having significantly different project costs (i.e. with capital rationing). The decision rule is to accept (reject) projects with PI greater (less) than 1.0. The firm's management is indifferent if PI = 1 as no value is created.

Example: Referring to our example project, the present value of cash inflows are equal to the present value of future cash flows from our NPV example: $1,475,480. (This will not be true if one of the project's future cash flows are negative, so be careful not to assume these two figures are always the same!) The present value of the cash outflows is equal to the investment: $750,000. PI = $1,475,480 / $750,000 = 1.97. This means that there is $0.97 in additional value for each $1 of investment. As long as PI is greater than 1, the firm increases in value if the project is undertaken. Since PI > 1, accept the proposed project.

Mutually exclusive projects

There are two decision types: (1) accept or reject a capital project; and, (2) capital rationing, wherein a decision-maker must select some set of capital projects among a larger set of worthwhile projects (i.e. not all projects can be undertaken because there is a limited supply of funds; some worthwhile projects will be unfunded). Up to this point, our discussion has been about the evaluation of a single project, or the funding of all available projects meeting the criterion of positive NPV or an IRR exceeding the hurdle rate. That is, we have been talking about decisions of the first type. In this section we discuss the second type of decision.

To illustrate the problem that develops when there is a limited supply of funds, assume that the firm has the example problem used throughout this chapter. But also assume that the hotel has a second project whose cash flows differ only with respect to the investment (i.e. at time $t = 0$) and the salvage value cash flow obtained at the end of Year 5 (i.e. the terminal value). For this second project, the investment is $575,000 and the salvage value will be $600,000. At a required rate of return of 10%, NPV for this second project is $745,249, a figure slightly above the first project. Accordingly, the second project is preferred to the first. IRR for this project is 43.8%, a value markedly above the first project. These two criteria appear to suggest that the second project is absolutely preferred to the first project.

But what if the required rate of return was something other than 10%? It turns out, if NPV for both projects is computed for different required rates of return, there is a point at which the first project is preferred. Figure 5.4 plots NPV for both projects over a range of required rates of return. The first project, represented by the solid line, it can be seen, is preferred when the required rate of return is less than approximately 7.4% and the second project (dashed line) is preferred at rates above 7.4%.

This result comes about because the first project has a significantly larger investment followed by a larger payout in the last year. At high required rates of return, the present value of the final cash flow is reduced significantly and it is "less able" to offset the project's relatively larger investment. The second project, because of its lower investment, does relatively better. Conversely, at low required rates of return, the final cash flow of the first project is not discounted heavily. Accordingly, the present value of the final cash flow adequately offsets the large investment. Again, these cash flows are relative when the firm has mutually exclusive projects.

The purpose of this section is to make explicit the fact that a selection, or ranking, of projects *depends on the firm's required rate of return*. And since the projects' rate of return varies for each firm, it is possible – even likely – that project rankings/priorities vary across firms even if the assumptions of future cash flows are the same.

When evaluating mutually exclusive projects, the decision is more challenging because: (1) of our assumption that the firm could re-invest its future cash flows at the required rate of return; and, (2) that an analyst can determine the firm's required rate of return.

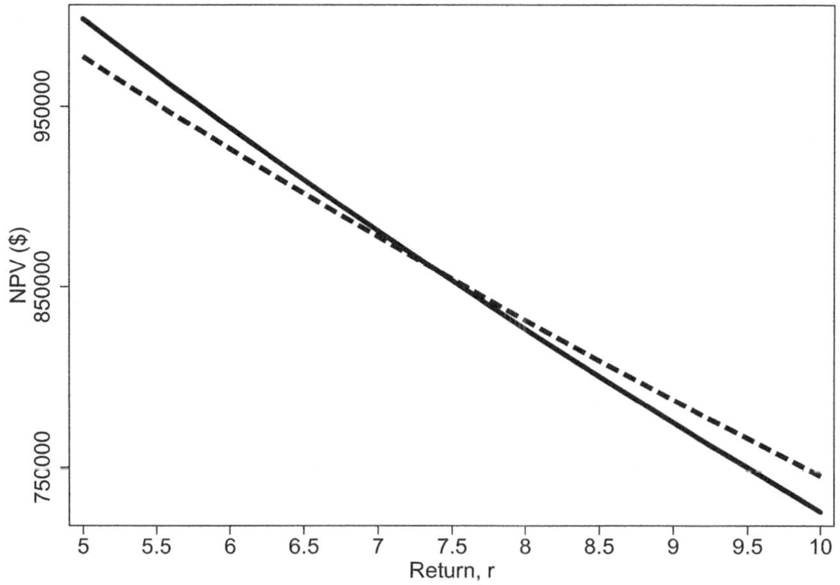

Figure 5.4 Net present value and required rate of return: mutually exclusive projects

Note: The solid line represents the first project. The dashed line represents the second project. The required rate of return, r, that both projects have equal NPV is approximately 7.4%.

Summary

In this chapter we examined issues and appraisal techniques that are used to plan and control long-term, capital investment. You should now understand:

1. How ongoing capital investment is critical for the long-term success of hospitality firms;
2. how to distinguish capital investment from repairs and maintenance expenditure, and how to account for these different expenditures;
3. the time value of money and how this applies to the investment appraisal methods commonly used (i.e. NPV, IRR, modified IRR, payback, modified payback, ARR, and PI); and,
4. the issues that arise when there are mutually exclusive projects.

Appendix: Unconventional cash flows

This appendix expands upon an important, if infrequent, issue that may occur when appraising investments using IRR. In cases where there are negative future cash flows, IRR can have more than one solution (i.e. multiple interest rates yield zero NPV). NPV is then preferred to IRR but, if the analyst still wants to use IRR, she must do so with caution. To illustrate the problem, assume a project with an investment of $1,600 and the following future, annual cash flows: $1,400, $1,400, $2,600, $2,500 and –$7,000. The last cash flow represents the cash flows from the final year of the project, plus the salvage value of the project assets at the end of the project life (in this case, the salvage value is sufficiently negative such that positive cash flows in the project's final year are wiped out by the larger, negative salvage value). One finds, perhaps with the assistance of Excel or a financial calculator, an IRR of 7.5%. If we assume management had a criterion of 15% for project acceptance, this project would be rejected. If we further assume that the firm's cost of capital is 10%, one obtains a net present value of $144.25. It seems counterintuitive that a higher discount rate (from 7.5% for IRR up to the 10% cost-of-capital rate) results in a positive NPV! Furthermore, a positive NPV means that the firm should accept the project. This is the opposite decision to that reached using IRR! Based on NPV, failing to accept the project means that the firm will forego an opportunity to create greater value for its owners. Since the IRR and NPV assessment techniques provide contradictory recommendations, how does one resolve the problem? More importantly, what's happening that leads us to this dilemma?

To better understand this, plot NPV for a range of discount rates (see Figure 5.5). This plot reveals that NPV rises rapidly, to a peak at a discount rate of about 28%, then falls slowly until NPV is zero at a discount rate of approximately 73.5%. If, as is evident here, there are two solutions for IRR, the decision criterion can appear to be ambiguous over a range of interest rates.

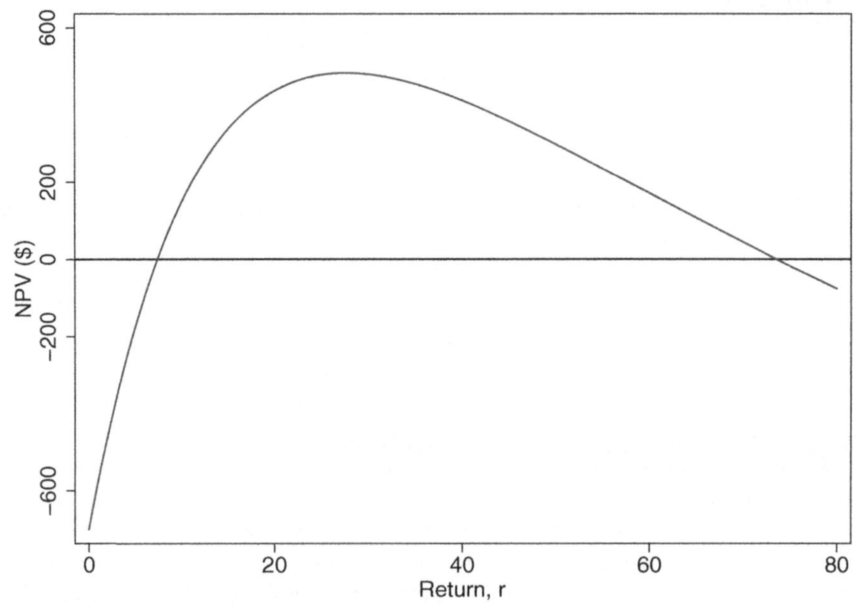

Figure 5.5 IRR for projects with unconventional cash flows

Basically, at low discount rates, the relatively large negative cash flow in the final period maintains a great deal of its value and this causes NPV to be negative. However, as discount rates increase above 7.5%, the future negative cash flow is discounted sufficiently such that the modest, positive cash flows in period 1–4 overcome the discounted present value of that final cash flow, and NPV becomes positive. However, as the discount rate goes beyond the second IRR solution (at 73.54%), the present values of the future cash flows are so heavily discounted that these cannot overcome the project's initial cash outlay (i.e. its investment). While this example has a large range of ambiguity, or conflict between NPV and IRR, a different scenario of cash flows could yield a much smaller range of conflict.

Another anomaly can be seen if one increases the cost of the initial investment – say from $1,600 to $1,900. Your intuition might lead you to think that IRR and NPV would both decrease. Indeed, NPV is lower for all discount rates. But the two solutions are now 13.8% and 49.8%. Despite an increase in investment – and no change in future cash flows – the IRR increased substantially, making the investment appear to be *more* attractive! In other words, if a hotel were to spend more on a renovation, it would earn a *higher* return! Obviously, this does not make sense, and we see that the IRR appraisal technique may lead the analyst to make bad decisions.

In sum, one must exercise caution when there are unconventional (i.e. negative) future cash flows. A better solution is to use the NPV appraisal technique as this method always provides the correct assessment. In situations where it's difficult to determine a firm's cost of capital, and where there are conventional cash flows, IRR is a suitable alternative.

Reference

ISHC (2024). *CapEx2023: A Study of Capital Expenditures in the Hotel Industry*, 6th edition. Atlanta, GA: *International Society of Hospitality Consultants.*

PRACTICE: INVESTING IN SUSTAINABILITY: THE CASE OF THE SS GAUKROGERS

Rob van Ginneken

Introduction

In this practice section, we look at how Hildifons Cruise Lines Inc. decided, in 2015, to invest in the modernisation of their flagship vessel, the SS Gaukrogers. More specifically, we show how Hildifons employed some of the capital budgeting concepts discussed in the theory part. Please note there are no such company and no such ship. This case has been developed using information from a number of hospitality renovation projects, in and outside of the cruise industry. This means you should not expect all technical and financial details to be 100% spot-on. The idea is to show the decision making "train of thought" of a real business. So just go with the flow (pun not intended) and learn more about this very important aspect of Finance and Accounting.

Hildifons Cruise Lines and the SS Gaukrogers

Hildifons is a cruise operator in South-East Asia. Its headquarters are in Singapore, and its seven ships sail the waters of the region, servicing ports such as Manila, Benoa Harbour (Bali, Indonesia) and Phu My (Ho Chi Minh City, Vietnam). The SS Gaukrogers was launched from dry-dock in 1982, making it Hildifons' oldest ship in the fleet. It carries 1,500 passengers and 500 crew members. At the time of launch it was considered state of the art, setting new standards in terms of both the physical product as well as guest services provided.

Over the years, several modernisation and renovation projects were carried out: the ventilation equipment in the early 90s; a new gym and banqueting facilities were created in 2007, also requiring more modern climate control. Most of the machinery and equipment was, however, original, still functioning after 33 years of solid maintenance, when Hildifons decided to retrofit the SS Gaukrogers in 2015. The company decided to invest in a major technical renovation project to bring the vessel to new levels of energy efficiency and comfort. A major reason for the decision was the increasing criticism attracted by the cruise industry from environmentalists. The carbon dioxide footprint of cruise vacations is large – even ignoring the fact that many guests will travel by plane to their port of departure. And it's not confined to just the CO_2 from fuel consumption: sulphur emissions are also a problem, which has led regulatory body International Maritime Organisation to require shippers to use lower-sulphur fuels as of 2020. Waste and (sometimes oil-contaminated) waste water is also an issue. In response to all of this, most if not all international cruise operators have formulated sustainability programs. These typically contain targets for reductions in fuel and utilities consumption. In the case of Hildifons, such a plan was announced in 2015. It focused on retrofitting older ships, that is, replacing substantial parts of a ship's hardware with modern-day technology. First up: the SS Gaukrogers.

The project

Shortly after the retrofit strategy was announced, the Hildifons finance team met with the ship's engineers and performed an analysis of the existing hardware. The following two main areas were identified as the ones with the highest potential in terms of both contributing to the company's sustainability targets and generating savings:

1. Retrofitting engines to have them run on liquefied natural gas (LNG) rather than diesel.
2. Using heat generated in the engine cooling process to generate warm water for guest use.

The heat-recovery project would obviously lead to energy savings. Using the "free" source of engine-generated heat means less energy would be needed to keep the ship's hot water supply (for showering for example) at the right temperature at all times. The biggest advantage from the LNG retrofit, from a sustainability perspective, is cleaner emissions: LNG is typically considered the cleanest-burning fossil fuel. For Hildifons, the economic advantages of this retrofit are many. To begin with, LNG is somewhat cheaper than diesel. Of course, that may change in the future; Hildifons finance team estimated future savings taking into account expected political (environmental regulation), economic and technological developments. On top of the projected fuel cost savings, Hildifons also expected the switch to LNG to generate substantial savings on fuel storage, technical maintenance, and environmental permits.

The numbers: Calculation of IRR and NPV

The total investment was (Singapore) $7,078,500, or just over $9,000 per cabin. The expected annual savings from the combined projects were $1,012,245:

- savings in fuel of $862,245 from the two projects combined;
- other savings based on the expected lower "total cost of ownership" of LNG versus diesel, of $150,000.

As the work was carried out in the first five months of 2017, the savings in that year are lower. Because savings increase pre-tax profit, they also increase taxes. In Singapore the corporate income tax rate is 17%. In Table 5.3 we see how Hildifons calculated taxes, taking the savings and the depreciation of the investment into account, and then determined the net after-tax effect of the investment on cash flow.

In Figure 5.6 these cash flow savings from the project are in the central part ("Cash flows (+000)". From Year 2, the "stabilised year" in which the new systems are fully operational, the figures increase by 2% per year to account for inflation (due to rounding, this is not clearly visible). The "Base case cash flow" refers to the situation in which the cruise line would not undertake this project, and hence would not generate any savings.

Table 5.3 From savings to after-tax cash flows

	2017 ($)	2018 ($)	2019 ($)	2020 ($)	2021 ($)	2022 ($)	2023 ($)
a: Savings	491,250	1,012,245	1,032,490	1,053,140	1,074,202	1,095,687	1,117,600
b: Depreciation of investment (investment / 20 years)	353,925	353,925	353,925	353,925	353,925	353,925	353,925
c: Corporate income tax (17% of a – b)	23,345	111,914	115,356	118,866	122,447	126,099	129,825
d: Cash flow (a – c)	467,905	900,331	917,134	934,273	951,755	969,587	987,775

Summary Return Analysis - SS Gaukrogers

Proposed Project - LNG & Heat Re-Use — ***Singapore dollars***

Project Returns (IRR)	
7 Years with Residual	**27.5%**

Key Assumptions	
Proforma Start Date	**Jan-17**
Construction Start Date	**Jan-17**
Construction End Date	**may-17**
Project Total Investment (+000)	**7,079**
Number of Cabins	**750**
Investment Per Cabin	**9**
Stabilized Inflation Rate	**2.0%**
Stabilized Year	**2**
Analysis Term (Years)	**7**

Residual Value		
Net of 1.5% transaction costs	**(+000)**	**Cap Rate**
Base Case Residual Value	**0**	**5.75%**
ROI Project Case Residual Value	**17,239**	**5.75%**
Incremental Residual Value	**17,239**	--

Cash Flows (+000)

	Year 1	*Year 2*	*Year 3*	*Year 4*	*Year 5*	*Year 6*	*Year 7*
	2017	2018	2019	2020	2021	2022	2023
Number of Days	365	365	365	366	365	365	365
Base Case Cash Flow	0	0	0	0	0	0	0
YOY % Change		-	-	-	-	-	-
ROI Project Case Cash Flow	468	900	917	934	952	970	988
YOY % change		*92.4%*	*1.9%*	*1.9%*	*1.9%*	*1.9%*	*1.9%*
Incremental cash flow	**468**	**900**	**917**	**934**	**952**	**970**	**988**
YOY % change		*92.4%*	*1.9%*	*1.9%*	*1.9%*	*1.9%*	*1.9%*

IRR Sensitivity Matrix

Total Investment	Residual cap rate **4.75%**	**5.25%**	**5.75%**	**6.25%**	**6.75%**
6,079	35.2%	33.5%	32.0%	30.7%	29.4%
6,267	34.3%	32.6%	31.1%	29.7%	28.5%
6,460	33.4%	31.7%	30.2%	28.8%	27.6%
6,660	32.5%	30.8%	29.3%	27.9%	26.7%
6,866	31.6%	29.9%	28.4%	27.0%	25.8%
7,079	30.7%	29.0%	27.5%	26.2%	25.0%
7,291	29.8%	28.1%	26.6%	25.3%	24.1%
7,510	29.0%	27.3%	25.8%	24.5%	23.3%
7,735	28.2%	26.5%	25.0%	23.7%	22.5%
7,967	27.3%	25.7%	24.2%	22.9%	21.7%
8,206	26.5%	24.9%	23.4%	22.1%	20.9%

Figure 5.6 ROI presentation

At the top left of the spreadsheet, you can see Hildifons calculated the IRR "with residual" for this project to be 27.5%. How did they arrive at this figure? First of all, all cash flows, as usual in capital budgeting, are assumed to take place at the end of the period (year). In this case, as the project work was carried out over the first five months of 2017, the investment of $7,078,500, just like all savings expected in that year, was assumed to have been made at the end of 2017. For those interested in Excel detail: Hildifons used the XIRR and XNPV functions which allow the analyst to exactly time the cash flows rather than the regular IRR and NPV which assume cash flows occur at regular intervals.

Then there's the section called "Residual value". Obviously, only using a seven-year time horizon for the calculation of project return is arbitrary. The savings are not going to stop all of a sudden, on New Year's Eve 2023. Theoretically, they could go on forever. But calculations involving infinity are difficult; for that reason, in exercises such as this, companies use what you could call a trick. The trick is they fictively assume they will sell the investment after a number of years. The price they would get for it is thought to be a multiple of how much cash flow the investment would generate in the year after the sale – in our example, that would be the savings in Year 8. Hildifons assumed a multiple here of roughly 17, or, as this is usually expressed, a so-called "cap rate" of 5.75%. In other words, if the fictive new owner would pay 17 times his first-year return for this investment, they would make a return in the first year of 5.75%. The total post-tax savings in year 8 (not in the table) were $1,006,328 – dividing that number by the cap rate of 0.0575 equates to a fictive selling price, or residual, of $17,501,350. From this, the costs associated with a sale – 1.5% of the selling price – are subtracted, to arrive at a fictive positive cash flow at the end of year 7 of $17,238,830. This was added to the savings cash flow of $987,775 in that year, making for a total Year 7 cash flow of $18,226,605.

The IRR sensitivity matrix is the last section on this Summary return analysis prepared for the SS Gaukrogers project. It offers the reader some additional insights into how sensitive the resulting IRR of this project is to changes in two assumptions, or input variables: the project cost and the estimated residual cap rate. In more common parlance: the figures in this table help in that they provide two "What if?" scenarios. For example, should the project turn out to cost $7,510 (,000) rather than the projected $7,079 (,000), or 6% more, then the IRR would drop to 25.8%. Nothing dramatic perhaps, but 6% is not a lot; as you will learn throughout your business career, the true costs of large investment projects often more significantly exceed the estimates! Should Hildifons decide to sell the ship after a few years, and should the selling price correspond to a cap rate of not 5.75, but rather 6.75% – i.e. a lower selling price – in combination with the project cost underestimation of $431,000, that would mean the overall IRR would drop to 23.3%. It seems this project is pretty robust.

As you know after having studied capital budgeting theory, the accept/reject criterion is the WACC (weighted average cost of capital) or any other hurdle rate set by the company for investment. In the case of Hildifons, this was set at 9%, the percentage used to also calculate the Net present value of the project – which was determined to be (again including the residual) $7,878,058. Needless to say, the company went on to make the investment.

Conclusion

In this last practice section, we have looked at an investment in sustainability with a clear impact on profitability through fuel consumption and other savings. This case is a nice example of rather *theoretical* concepts such as IRR and NPV actually being part of the toolbox used by hospitality *professionals*. However, we should take into consideration that Hildifons is a large professional hospitality business. The use of capital budgeting techniques in smaller businesses may very well be much less sophisticated, perhaps even more intuitive.

Notes

1 For example, if the manager expects to easily achieve this year's performance target, she will treat the expenditure as an expense item. She'll receive her bonus this year and, without future depreciation expense, accounting income in future years will be higher, increasing the likelihood of future bonuses. On the other hand, if she thinks there is a possibility the bonus target will be difficult to meet (but still likely), she'll capitalise the expenditure to minimise the impact on this year's accounting income. Finally, if her budget target is impossible to meet, she'll treat the expenditure as an expense item because this year's bonus is already lost. This example clearly illustrates that incentive compensation considerations drive managerial decision-making!

2 As this topic is beyond the scope of an introductory text, interested readers should refer to a finance text.

3 The payback period can also be expressed as something other than years (e.g. months, days or even hours). But since capital budgeting is a long-term investment, it is common to use years. This results in the payback period typically being a non-integer value.

Index

Page numbers in *italics* refer to figures and page numbers followed by 'n' refer to notes.

For Product Safety Concerns and Information please contact our EU representative GPSR@taylorandfrancis.com Taylor & Francis Verlag GmbH, Kaufingerstraße 24, 80331 München, Germany

Printed and bound by CPI Group (UK) Ltd, Croydon, CR0 4YY
06/02/2026
02049561-0011